D0891570

Understanding
CLAUDE SIMON

UNDERSTANDING MODERN EUROPEAN and LATIN AMERICAN LITERATURE

JAMES HARDIN, *SERIES EDITOR*

ADVISORY BOARD

* * * * *

Understanding Günter Grass
by Alan Frank Keele

Understanding Graciliano Ramos
by Celso Lemos de Oliveira

Understanding Gabriel García Márquez
by Kathleen McNerney

Understanding Claude Simon
by Ralph Sarkonak

UNDERSTANDING

CLAUDE
SIMON

by RALPH SARKONAK

UNIVERSITY OF SOUTH CAROLINA PRESS

LIBRARY OF CONGRESS
Library of Congress Cataloging-in-Publication Data

Sarkonak, Ralph William, 1949–
    Understanding Claude Simon / Ralph Sarkonak.
      p.   cm.—(Understanding Modern European and Latin
    American Literature)
    Includes bibliographical references.
    ISBN 0–87249–669–4
    1. Simon, Claude—Criticism and interpretation. I. Title.
  II. Series.
PQ2637.I547Z86   1989
843′.914—dc20   89–16741
                                                      CIP

CONTENTS

EDITOR'S PREFACE

Understanding Modern European and Latin American Literature has been planned as a series of guides for undergraduate and graduate students and nonacademic readers. Like its companion series, *Understanding Contemporary American Literature,* the aim of the books is to provide an introduction to the life and writings of prominent modern authors and to explicate their most important works.

Modern literature makes special demands, and this is particularly true of foreign literature, in which the reader must contend not only with unfamiliar, often arcane artistic conventions and philosophical concepts, but also with the handicap of reading the literature in translation. It is a truism that the nuances of one language can be rendered in another only imperfectly (and this problem is especially difficult in fiction), but the fact that the works of European and Latin American writers are situated in a historical and cultural setting quite different from our own can be as great a hindrance to the understanding of these works as the linguistic barrier. For this reason, the UMELL series will emphasize the sociological and historical background of the writers treated. The peculiar philosophical and cultural traditions of a given culture may be particularly important for an understanding of certain authors, and these will be taken up in the introductory chapter and also in the discussion of those works to which this information is relevant. Beyond this, the books will treat the specifically literary aspects of the author under discussion and attempt to explain the complexities of contemporary literature lucidly. The books are conceived as introductions to the authors covered, not as comprehensive analyses. They do not provide detailed summaries of plot as they are meant to be used in conjunction with the books they treat, not as a substitute for the study of the original works. It is our hope that the UMELL series will help to increase our knowledge and understanding of the European and Latin American cultures and will serve to make the literature of those cultures more accessible.

Professor Sarkonak's *Understanding Claude Simon* is a lively, perceptive study of a writer whose works "travel" well, but about whom we know too little. This volume goes a long way toward correcting that deficiency.

J.H.

PREFACE

Since World War II, Claude Simon has published thirteen novels and half a dozen other works, including his acceptance speech for the Nobel Prize for Literature which he won in 1985. I have chosen to discuss the novels of Simon in chronological order, beginning with the first one to be translated into English, *Le Vent* (*The Wind*). This novel is important not because it is the author's best but because it provides readers who wish to familiarize themselves with Simon's *oeuvre* an excellent introduction to the author's style of writing at a time when it was still relatively traditional. In the nine novels that Simon wrote over the next twenty-four years, his style was to change radically, although many of the themes portrayed changed little during that time. For this reason, it is best to read the novels in the order in which they were originally published, for each novel leads to the next one.

I have quoted from the English-language translations of the novels but have also followed those page references with page references to the original French versions. When, for reasons of clarity or greater accuracy I have altered the published translation, the emendation is indicated following the relevant quotation. In the case of Simon's 1981 novel, *Les Géorgiques,* the translations are my own.

It remains for me to thank Susan Bree and Bruce Ferguson for their help with the bibliography and in general for keeping me on my toes. I should also like to thank Alistair MacKay and Charles Porter for their invaluable advice and encouragement.

Oct. 10, 1913	Born of French parents in Tananarive, Madagascar, where his father, an officer in the Colonial Army, was stationed.
1914	Death of Simon's father, killed in one of the first battles of World War I.
1924	Death of Simon's mother.
1920s	Secondary education in Perpignan and later Paris at the prestigious Collège Stanislas.
1930s	Studied painting with André Lhote; traveled throughout Europe.
1934–35	Military service in the French army.
1936	Sojourn in Barcelona during the Spanish Civil War.
1939	Recalled to active duty in his old cavalry regiment (31st Dragoons).
May 1940	Taken prisoner of war during the Battle of the Meuse. POW in Germany; transferred to a camp in France.
Nov. 1940	Escaped from POW camp.
1945	Publication of *Le Tricheur* (completed in 1941).

| 1947 | *La Corde raide.* |

1952   *Gulliver.*

1954   *Le Sacre du printemps.*

1957   *Le Vent,* Simon's first novel to be published by Les Editions de Minuit.

1958   *L'Herbe.*

1959   Publication of *The Wind,* Simon's first book to be translated into English.

1960   *La Route des Flandres.*
Received the Prix de *L'Express* for *La Route des Flandres*
Signed the "Manifesto of the 121" on the right of French conscripts to disobey their officers during the Algerian conflict.

1962   *Le Palace.*

1966   *Femmes,* text by Simon on 23 paintings by Joan Miró.

1967   *Histoire.*
Received the Prix Médicis for *Histoire.*

1969   *La Bataille de Pharsale.*

1970   *Orion aveugle.*

1971	*Les Corps conducteurs.*
1973	*Triptyque.*
1975	*Leçon de choses.*
1981	*Les Géorgiques.*
1983	*La Chevelure de Bérénice,* reprint of Simon's text in *Femmes.*
1985	Received the Nobel Prize for Literature.
1986	*Discours de Stockholm.* Visit to U.S.S.R. in company of fourteen other international personalities, including James Baldwin and Peter Ustinov.
1987	*L'Invitation.*
1988	*Album d'un amateur.*
1989	*L'Acacia*

Understanding
CLAUDE SIMON

> Claude Simon's narrative art may appear as a rep-
> resentation of something that lives within us
> whether we will it or not, whether we understand it
> or not—something hopeful, in spite of all the cruelty
> and absurdity which seem to characterize our condi-
> tion and which are so perceptively, penetratingly
> and abundantly reproduced in his novels.[1]

These are the words used by the jury to describe the
oeuvre of Claude Simon when it awarded him the Nobel Prize for Literature in 1985. Twenty-one years after
Jean-Paul Sartre refused the Nobel awarded to him,
Simon, whose novels have been translated into eighteen languages, became the eleventh French writer to
receive the famous prize. But Simon was then and still
is anything but famous. In fact, when the 1985 Nobel
Prize winner was announced, the literary establish-
ment in Europe and America was hard put to characterize Simon's writing to members of the press. As one
journalist wrote, "Some people tried to get information
about Mr. Simon. Some tried to fake it. A few cognoscenti were in the coveted position of being able to
argue the merits of the choice. Others merely
shrugged."[2] One writer wondered whether Claude Simon was a man or a woman, while others claimed to
have socialized with Mr. Simon at parties in Manhat-
tan and the Hamptons. Upon being told that Simon is
somewhat of a recluse, Calvin Trillin replied "Susan

Sontag better have heard of this guy or there'll be trouble."[3] A professor at a well-known American university described Simon in the following terms, which are not entirely accurate. "Many people who are literate, even those who read *The New York Times Book Review,* haven't registered the name. He's never written anything scandalous or won a major prize or made himself the talk of the town. He's just been there for 30 years."[4] In fact, Simon won two prestigious literary prizes in France, the Prix de *L'Express* in 1960 and the Prix Médicis in 1967. In 1960 during the Algerian War, his signing of the "Manifesto of the 121," a petition inciting French conscripts to desert, as well as his subsequent disagreement with Sartre's conception of literature and writing, had not gone unnoticed, at least not in European intellectual circles. On the other hand, Simon fared little better in his own country where one critic was moved to wonder if by awarding the Nobel to him the jury wanted "to confirm the rumor that the novel has definitely died," as Simon himself mischievously pointed out in his acceptance speech before the assembled dignitaries in Stockholm.[5] No doubt the most intelligent reaction recorded was that of a librarian at the New York Public Library who stated, "You can say, it's all right to be ignorant. But it's not all right to remain ignorant."[6]

Who then is this "illustrious unknown" who has published some 20 books over a period of 42 years? Claude Eugène Henri Simon was born in Madagascar of French parents on October 10, 1913.[7] His father, a cavalry officer, was killed at the very beginning of World War I in 1914, and Simon's mother died when he was 11. He grew up in the south of France in Perpignan and in Salses in a house which he still owns. He studied in Perpignan and later at a Catholic boarding school in Paris, the Collège Stanislas. He was also a sometime university student at Oxford and Cambridge, although his only degree is the honorary one he received from the University of East Anglia in 1973. Simon has long been interested in the visual arts and early on he tried his hand at painting. He gave it up when he realized that he lacked the necessary technical skills. His sympathies for the Republican side drew him to Spain in 1936 at the time of the civil war. At the onset of war in 1939, he was drafted into a cavalry regiment, the 31st Dragoons, that was sent to the same area of the front "where, [2]6 years earlier, my father had been killed."[8] In the spring of 1940, Simon was taken prisoner during the Battle of the Meuse and sent to a prisoner-of-war camp in Germany. He managed to get himself transferred to a POW camp in France from which he escaped in November 1940. After his escape he joined the resistance movement in Perpignan.

In 1945 he published his first work, an untranslated novel entitled *Le Tricheur* (The Cheat). Today Simon divides his time between his home in Salses and an apartment in the Latin Quarter of Paris. Until the award of the Nobel Prize, Simon had earned little money from his writing;[9] he lived on income from his wine-growing on the estate he inherited from his mother's side of the family. One of his favorite pastimes is making huge collages, and the patchwork-quilt technique of writing has remained a constant in his method of composing, despite the evolution in the various styles he has adopted over the years. Simon continues to write and recently published a short text describing a trip to the USSR, including a fictionalized account of a meeting with Mikhail Gorbachev.[10] Now at age seventy-five, Simon has just had published another major novel, *L'Acacia*.[11]

Never given to abstract theorizing about his own fiction, Simon has often stated in interviews and lectures that he is not a writer with a special message. In fact, he gave the following description of his life and his "philosophy" in his acceptance speech for the Nobel Prize:

Now I am an old man and, like many of the inhabitants of old Europe, the first part of my life was quite eventful: I was witness to a revolution; I was a soldier in conditions that were particularly lethal (I belonged to one of those regiments which staff officers coldly sacrifice in advance so that almost nothing of it remained after a week); I was taken prisoner; I knew hunger, physical work leading to exhaustion; I escaped; I have been seriously ill, several times on the brink of a violent or natural death; I have rubbed shoulders with the most diverse people, priests as well as arsonists who burn down churches, peaceful middle-class citizens as well as anarchists, philosophers as well as illiterates; I have shared my daily bread with criminals; finally I have traveled almost everywhere in the world ... however, I have not yet discovered, at age 72, any meaning to all of this, unless it is, as I believe [Roland] Barthes said after Shakespeare, that "if the world means anything, it's that it doesn't mean anything"—except that it is. (24)

Simon is one of a group of French writers whose careers got underway after World War II and whose aesthetics, though not identical, constitute a reaction to the dual tradition of social and psychological realism that characterized novel-writing in France between the wars and which even today remains the preserve of many conventional novelists.[12] Although his novels are often associated with the so-called New Novel— other members of this school of writing include Marguerite Duras (1914–) and Alain Robbe-Grillet (1922–) —in fact when Simon speaks of his own works, he tends to mention the names of innovative writers born in the nineteenth century. These include Feodor Dostoyevsky (1821–81), Marcel Proust (1871–1922), James Joyce (1882–1941), and William Faulkner (1897–1962), all of whom had a considerable influence upon him. It is not by chance that only one Frenchman appears in the list cited since Simon feels his writing has little in common with the classic tradition of the French novel as it has evolved since the seventeenth century, culminating in the works of Simon's least favorite *bêtes noires,* André Malraux (1901–76) and Jean-Paul Sartre (1905–80). Unlike these two writers, Simon has never claimed to have discovered any earth-shattering truths about life. In fact, he has gone so far as to state that "ultimately there is nothing to say."[13]

If this is the case, one might well ask why he has written so much and why he continues to write. Simon has addressed this question in terms which might appear naïve but which in fact lie at the very heart of his understanding and practice of the art of the novel. "If I have written (and still write), it is very prosaically, and maybe very selfishly, because I was impelled (as everyone is in his field, I think) by a certain need of 'doing.'"[14] And in his acceptance speech in Stockholm, he gave his own version of the famous Cartesian *cogito:* "I make—I produce—, therefore I am" (23). The idea of the writer as maker is, of course, hardly a new one since the word *poet* is derived from the Greek verb *poiein* "to make." Simon sees himself as a maker of verbal objects, a poet, albeit one who writes in prose. He is not ashamed of the fact that he works hard at his writing. The stereotypical image of the writer feverishly composing under the guidance of some divine muse, of the writer who covers pages and pages of blank paper effortlessly, of the writer who lets his pen take him where his characters lead him is seen by Simon, with his many years of writing experience, as arrant nonsense that doesn't correspond to the reality of the writer's craft. If some readers of his novels have denounced them as the products of "laborious" and "artificial" work, Simon himself is highly conscious of the hard work that has gone into them and does not seek to hide the fact.[15] On the contrary, he sees no reason why an artist, just like any other worker, whether manual or intellectual, should not be proud of his or her labors. Of course, this kind of novel-writing supposes that the author's readers will be willing to put the necessary effort into "deciphering" the text.

Simon has the reputation of being a difficult writer. In fact, when his novels are properly understood, they are highly enjoyable. As one critic puts it, "In [Simon's] novels the rich sensuality and luxuriance of physical detail, the delicate arrangement of mass and shadow, the melancholy but often sumptuous appraisal of man's fleeting destiny turn the passageways of what might seem arid research into stretches of pure enjoyment."[16] To be sure, his novels are not pulp fiction. On the other hand, he is a writer who is concerned with the real world, its history and geography, its shapes and colors, and—most of all—with life and death. In fact, Claude Simon is one of the most concrete and down-to-earth of modern French writers. Hence the significance of the manifold descriptions in his books. For Simon, to produce meaning by stringing words together one after the other is a constant challenge, for he is not content just to *label* "the world about us," to quote the English title of a recent novel of his. Rather he seeks to (re)produce the world by the use of descriptions of intricate and beautiful detail. The pleasure of reading Simon's novels is considerable, and a large part of that pleasure lies in the author's ability to create an entire fictive universe in and through the descriptive resources of language.

Of course, Simon's novels are not conventional narratives. This is why a purely thematic approach to his art is not entirely satisfying. On the other hand, Simon is not a writer of science fiction or of tales of the supernatural. His texts are grounded in the daily experiences of ordinary life, which for him usually includes love and war. However, whether or not readers took part in, or are familiar with other narratives about, the Spanish Civil War is immaterial, for in reading Simon's descriptions of wartorn Barcelona in *The Palace, Histoire,* and *The Georgics,* we "recognize" the world about which we are reading. Even such apparently fantastical passages as those that describe the transformation of two lovers caught *in flagrante delicto* into a stone sculpture in *The Battle of Pharsalus* can

9

be read as extended developments or expansions inspired by a figure of speech, here of the expression "to
be *petrified* with fear."

Simon is a writer who loves to describe objects and
people, and in fact it would be quite accurate to say
that he paints with his pen. More often than not the
human characters he describes are not given greater
importance than the inanimate objects which surround
them, just as in a collage all the images or objects that
go into it exist on the same level, whatever their prove-
nance, monetary value, or intrinsic artistic "worth."
On the other hand, Simon's novels do describe typical
human dramas in terms which are remarkably poignant. Contrary to what some readers who have read
Simon only superficially may think, his novels are not
dry or dull, nor are they restricted to readers who have
acquired a familiarity with French critical theory of
the 1960s and 1970s, although the resources of literary
semiotics have been brought to bear on them.[17]

How then should one go about reading Simon? To a
certain extent learning to read Simon involves
unlearning many of the reading habits we have all
acquired in school and college. First of all, every traditional notion about plot and character one might think
of is successfully challenged and graphically over-
turned by his writing practice. Nevertheless, in their
unique way, the novels tell great stories. But readers
of Simon soon discover they are not playing with a full
deck of cards, so to speak, since all his texts tell tales
that are as incomplete and as untidy as life usually is.
Historical truth or veracity appears only as an elusive
and unattainable entity, a fictitious construct invented
by man to reassure himself in the face of a world made

up of unbearable uncertainty and perpetual transformation. In fact, the only definitive or ultimate truth in Simon's novels takes the form of the writing, the material words set down upon the page we are reading. In deciphering these narratives, reader participation is of prime importance. To read well is always to read actively (preferably with pen or computer at hand to take notes), but in the case of Simon, it becomes absolutely necessary if anything interesting and significant is to be discovered. On the other hand, readers should not expect to fully comprehend everything in these texts at first reading since the quest for knowledge in Simon is a gradual *process*. And while some gaps will be filled in progressively, others will remain always.

Readers should not be put off by Simon's innovative use of language. For example, in many, though not all of Simon's novels, he does not use conventional punctuation. Sentences may begin with a lowercase letter and end without the traditional period. He makes frequent use of parentheses and of parentheses within parentheses. (The longest one, in *The Georgics,* is thirty pages long in the French edition of the novel, but most are shorter than a page.) On the other hand, Simon takes care to help readers find their way through his sometimes labyrinthine syntax by his innovative use of typography, including the three dots which are the traditional symbol for ellipsis.[18] In Simon, three dots can indicate not only a break but also the continuation of an earlier narrative thread when they occur at the beginning of a paragraph. Often words and entire phrases are repeated in order to indicate a return to a previous theme, leitmotif or story line which has been temporarily displaced by another one, for two of the most significant effects that he seeks in his writing are simultaneity and superimposition. For example, life and death, love and war, tend to overlap and even to coalesce in the Simonian worldview. What is especially important is that such a point of view is made concrete by the details of the narratives up to and including the level of their stylistic fabric.

This raises the larger questions of textual ambiguity and structure. Whether it is a question of ambiguous pronoun references or a larger blurring of distinctions between characters or even entire historical epochs, everything recalls everything else. No doubt the reader's first impression will be of fragmentation and discontinuity. But closer examination of the texts will lead to the realization that they are intricately structured, although for the most part not ordered chronologically. While composing *The Flanders Road,* Simon used a system of colors to help him keep track of the interplay of times, places, characters, and themes.[19] Often his novels have an underlying geometrical or even a geological structure to them.[20] And in *The World About Us,* the ordering of the text and the interweaving of the various scenes recall the structure of a fugue.

In Simon, structure is always part and parcel of meaning, as it is in poetry. In fact, given the novelist's attention to cadence and word play, including rhyme, as well as his overall love for the sound and feel of language, his texts could well be considered prose poems. A further poetic element can be found in the self-reflexive character of Simon's novels, since in its own particular way each one refers to and describes itself.

Beginnings are especially significant in this regard since they contain numerous clues, not only as to the subject matter of the novel the reader is embarking upon, but also as to how it is constructed. It would not be an exaggeration to say that Simon's novels fulfill a pedagogical function since they teach us how to read them all the while we are engaged in the actual process of doing so. Hence, although the novels themselves are not the only commentary it is possible to make on these vibrant texts, no doubt they will always remain the best one.

NOTES

1. Nobel jury quoted by Guy P. Buchholtzer, "A poetic look at the fragility of life," *Globe and Mail* (Jan. 18, 1986): C8.

2. Maureen Dowd, "Nobel Panel's Pick Keeps Cognoscenti Guessing," *New York Times* (Oct. 18, 1985): 20.

3. Quoted by Dowd.

4. Ibid.

5. Quoted by Claude Simon, *Discours de Stockholm* (Paris: Minuit, 1986), p. 15. Other references will appear in the text; translations are my own.

6. Quoted by Dowd.

7. No booklength biography of Simon has been published to date. John Fletcher has written about the relationship between Simon's life and his works on several occasions: see the biographical note to *Claude Simon and Fiction Now* (London: Calder and Boyars, 1975), pp. 15–18; "Claude Simon: Autobiographie et fiction," *Critique* 414 (1981): 1211–17; as well as his introduction to *The Flanders Road* (London: Calder, 1985). Reproductions of some of the photos and postcards used by Simon in his writing can be found in *Entretiens,* ed. Marcel Séguier (Rodez: Subervie, 1972); Jean Ricardou, *Le Nouveau Roman* (Paris: Seuil, 1973); and Lucien Dällenbach, *Claude Simon* (Paris: Seuil, 1988).

8. Quoted by Michel Braudeau, "For Simon, Novels' Key is 'Plea-

sure,'" *New York Times* (Nov. 4, 1985): C15. Whether Braudeau's or Simon's error, the figure quoted is sixteen, which is obviously wrong.

9. The year Simon was awarded the Nobel, the prize money was worth the equivalent of $225,000.

10. Claude Simon, *L'Invitation* (Paris: Minuit, 1987).

11. Conversation with the author (May 8, 1988). An extract of this work in progress was published in French and English under the title "Fragment" in *Claude Simon: New Directions: Collected Papers,* ed. Alastair Duncan (Edinburgh: Scottish Academic P, 1985), pp. 2–11.

12. For an introduction to Simon's place in twentieth-century French literature, see J. A. E. Loubère, *The Novels of Claude Simon* (Ithaca and London: Cornell UP, 1975), pp. 13–45.

13. Quoted in anonymous article, "Nobel leaves him speechless," *Globe and Mail* (Oct. 18, 1985): A8. In a speech given at New York University in 1982, Simon explained his having "nothing to say" in the following terms: "I am [. . .] neither a philosopher [. . .], a moralist, or a believer. That is why I have nothing special to reveal about the great questions which are posed by mankind, like sex, the meaning of History, of life, evil or good" (*Three Decades of the French New Novel,* ed. Lois Oppenheim [Urbana: University of Illinois P, 1986], p. 83).

14. Claude Simon, New York Speech in *Three Decades of the French New Novel,* p. 73.

15. The words in quotes are Simon's own; cf. *Discours de Stockholm,* p. 12.

16. Loubère, *The Novels of Claude Simon,* pp. 35–36.

17. Celia Britton quite correctly states: "His novels are [. . .] in some ways the opposite of the usual stereotype of the *nouveau roman.* They are certainly not the schematic, rationalistic, over-intellectualized productions popularly associated with Robbe-Grillet or Butor, for instance" (*Claude Simon: Writing the Visible* [Cambridge, Eng.: Cambridge UP, 1987], p. 166).

18. In the present study, three dots in square brackets, [. . .], indicate that I have omitted part of a quoted passage; three dots without brackets reproduce Simon's text.

19. Cf. André Bourin, "Techniciens du roman: Claude Simon," *Nouvelles Littéraires* (Dec. 29, 1960): 4; Madeleine Chapsal, "Claude Simon" in *Quinze écrivains* (Paris: Julliard, 1963), p. 167.

20. See Claude Simon, "La fiction mot à mot," in *Nouveau Roman: hier, aujourd'hui 2. Pratiques,* ed. Jean Ricardou and Françoise Van Rossum-Guyon (Paris: UGE, 1972), pp. 73–97.

CHAPTER ONE

The Wind
(*Le Vent*)

The Wind, first published in French in 1957, is Claude Simon's fourth novel and his fifth book. Three other novels, *Le Tricheur* (The Cheat) (completed in 1941 and published in 1945), *Gulliver* (1952), and *Le Sacre du printemps* (Rite of Spring, 1954), as well as a nonfiction memoir, *La Corde raide* (The Tightrope, 1947), have not been translated into English, and indeed only *Gulliver* and *Le Sacre du printemps* are still available in French. These early works are primarily of interest to specialists who see in them prefigurations and anticipations of his later, more mature texts. The novels up to and including *The Wind* are fictionally independent in that they do not make use of the technique of reappearing characters which Simon was to use so effectively beginning in 1958 with *The Grass.*

And so *The Wind* is important as a transitional text. It was the last of Simon's early novels; it was the first of his novels to be published by the Editions de Minuit—the French publishing house known for such experimental writers as Samuel Beckett (1906–) and Alain Robbe-Grillet (1922–)—which led to Simon's being included in the group of novelists known collectively as the Midnight School (from the name of his new publisher) and the *Nouveau Roman* (the French

"New Novel," a critical term initially made popular by Robbe-Grillet and later by the critic and novelist, Jean Ricardou [1932–]).[1] In this novel, the author's prose demonstrates a distinctive texture which he will go on to perfect in the novels that follow the 1957 text in a steady progression. Since at this early stage of his career Simon did not use recurring characters, *The Wind* can be read and enjoyed without reading any of the texts that preceded it. On the other hand, many of the themes and techniques with which Simon was later to experiment find their way into *The Wind*. Reading this novel is like looking at a gallery of paintings from an artist's first period or manner. Good or not, they can but prepare us for what follows.

The Wind tells the story of Antoine Montès, a somewhat simple 35-year-old outsider, who shortly after World War II arrives in a town in the south of France where his father has recently died; because of his parents' estrangement before his birth, he has never himself been there. Thus he "returns" to a geographical area and a culture which he does not know although he has many links with it. Montès, who is not cunning or aggressive or even practical, becomes entangled in a series of legal battles and personal problems with a cast of unsavory characters. The steward who managed his father's property, a vineyard of enormous potential value that has been allowed to go to waste, soon comes to physical and legal blows with Montès; but this is the least of his worries. He is far more preoccupied by the fate of Rose, one of the workers in the cheap hotel where he stays, and her two daughters to whom he becomes very attached, even though none of them ever voices the deep love they all feel for one another. At the same time, in another part of town, and at a completely different level of society, the family of Montès's uncle is troubled by the sudden appearance of their woebegone relative, all the more so since the younger daughter, Cécile, who looks more like a boy than most of her boyfriends, falls in love with Montès. A gypsy boxer-cum-small time crook and Montès's matronly niece, Hélène, form a strange alliance thereby providing the link between the two love stories (Montès and Rose; Montès and Cécile), and this leads to a tragic outcome when the ex-boxer kills Rose and then himself. The social worker only allows Montès to see the children once, which causes him as much or more pain than the death of Rose, the only woman he ever loved.

The title of the novel refers not to just any kind of wind, but to a particular wind which blows for months at a time in the south of France (either the Mistral or, as is more likely, the Tramontane). Just as the city where most of the action of the novel takes place is not named, so too the wind is not specifically identified. *The Wind* is, of course, an evocative title, since one thinks of the American potboiler *Gone with the Wind* (1936) by Margaret Mitchell (1900–49) whose title in French is *Autant en emporte le vent*. Simon's title also alludes to *Wuthering Heights* (1847) by Emily Brontë (1818–48), which is translated in French as *Les Hauts de Hurlevent*. *Le Vent* can rightly be considered Simon's rewriting of these conventional titles, just as it is an attempt to write a "new novel."

Whereas the title of the novel refers to a natural force, its subtitle, "Attempt to restore a Baroque altarpiece" (not translated in the American edition), puts the emphasis squarely on human activities. To restore

18

a baroque altar-piece is a doubly human endeavor since first of all it had to be built, and later, perhaps hundreds of years later, someone attempts to restore the painting to its original splendor. Throughout his career, Simon has continued to be fascinated with painting.[2] His debt to the visual arts is here openly acknowledged. In terms of *The Wind,* who is the model? Who the artist? Who the restorer? Given the strange and complicated adventures that the principal character gets himself into, not to mention his Christ-like innocence, it seems fitting to imagine Montès as the central figure, or rather the model for the painting of the "saint" in the central panel of the altar-piece. Given the nonsexual but deep love that unites Montès with Rose, one could also imagine a painting of this oddball but saintly couple as a modern version of Christ and the Madonna. Such paintings often took the form of a triptych, an artistic form that Simon was to use as a structural model in later novels, in which the two outer panels might when folded inward cover the central one. Here, the outer panels could correspond, on the one hand, to Rose's two daughters who love and are loved by Montès and, on the other, to Cécile, who also loves him. When folded in, the backs of the two exterior panels could portray such lesser characters as the notary, the donator of the entire piece, and Montès's rich uncle known as the "fat man," both of whom are typical members of the French bourgeoisie who play secondary but necessary roles in the drama as it unfolds. They would also have the money to pay for such a painting!

As for the painter, one can identity him with the anonymous first-person narrator. One can appreciate the importance of the adjective used to describe the style of the altar-piece mentioned in the novel's French subtitle, "baroque." In French, the word means not only a particular period in the history of art (a seventeenth-century style characterized by elaborate, asymmetrical, flamboyant structures, whether in music, art, or literature), but also "bizarre," "strange"—as the characters and the story will prove to be, especially to any reader who is expecting an ordinary story presented in a matter-of-fact, chronological manner.

Finally there is the restorer. His or her work is hard, painstaking and demands complete devotion to the task at hand. Working step by step, to restore a chipped piece of paint here or to remove some unsightly varnish or even to fix the hinges joining the three panels of the painting, the restorer attempts a difficult and time-consuming task which in the end may prove impossible or at least less than successful. Here it is easy to draw a parallel with readers of Simon who must work at putting things together in the novel, making sure that it all fits, as they work with the basic materials which the original painter-cum-writer has provided. Thus the challenge is there, like a puzzle waiting to be put together, or to be more exact, like a series of broken fragments, of bits and pieces of a story (or of many) which readers can begin piecing together, "a sort of plesiosauric reality [to be] reconstructed out of fragments."[3]

The novel begins as follows:

"An idiot, that's all. Nothing but a fool, an imbecile. And everything you could say or suppose or try to deduce or explain only confirms what you could

see at first glance anyway: just an idiot, plain and
simple. Except they let this one walk around loose
and talk to people and sign papers and set off catastrophes. Because apparently doctors classify men
like him as harmless." (9, 9)

From the outset we are plunged into the middle of the
fictional events and, what is more, the middle of an
interpretation of those events as perceived by a person
whose identity we do not yet know. Although it is not
yet clear what kind of idiot we are dealing with, it is
obvious that the speaker perceives him to represent a
danger to others and to the order of society—he supposedly sets off catastrophes. If the speaker had his way,
the idiot would be locked up, not to protect or care for
him, but to protect those about him whom he apparently harms. One wonders just how great this danger
really is since the idiot just walks around, talks to
people, and signs papers. The reader begins to form
an opinion about the speaker, about his desire to lock
up people who may deviate from the norms of the society of which he is a member. Later on, we will be able
to identify the person who wants the idiot locked up
as a notary—a fitting representative of societal norms
given the notary's role in the conveyance of property
in France—the person quoting or reproducing his
words as the (first-person) narrator and the idiot as
Montès. From the vantage point of language, it is important to notice the use of parallel syntactic structures: "And everything you could say or suppose or try
to deduce or explain." Stylistically, the technique of
accumulating quasi synonyms is typical of Simon's
style. From the outset the tone is similar to many of

the dialogues in this and other Simonian novels: the complaining voice of a malcontent harps on some problematic question which (almost) defies verbalization. Despite the apparent disorder of the speaker's speech, it is in fact inlaid with literary echoes beginning with the first words. There is, of course, a reference to *The Idiot* (1868) by the Russian novelist Feodor Dostoyevsky which Simon has admitted he sought to "remake" in writing *The Wind*.[4] Furthermore, there is, of course, an allusion to Shakespeare's *Macbeth:*

> Life's but a walking shadow; a poor player,
> That struts and frets his hour upon the stage,
> And then is heard no more: it is a tale
> Told by an idiot, full of sound and fury,
> Signifying nothing. (5.5.24–28)

The quotation, which gave the title to a novel that has had considerable influence on Simon's writing, *The Sound and the Fury* (1929) by William Faulkner, raises the distinct possibility that the real idiot is not the person being talked about but the notary himself, the teller of the tale. By analogy one can then deduce that the Simonian narrator is also an idiot for undertaking such a hazardous enterprise as attempting to recount a story "full of sound and fury, / Signifying nothing."

The cast of characters in *The Wind* is a motley group. The notary is a hard-nosed businessman who is trying to cheat Montès out of the dilapidated but potentially rich property that he has inherited from his father. In addition, the notary plays the role of the chorus (as in an ancient Greek tragedy), since he makes comments about the activities of the various characters and gives voice to the opinions of the town:

"being instead a medium that seemed to speak not in his own behalf but for the whole town" (114, 108). We learn relatively little about the listener to the notary's initial diatribe who is also the first-person narrator of the novel. He is a high school teacher interested in Romanesque churches, on which he is writing a book, and photography, an interest he shares with Montès.

As for Montès himself, he is a kind of innocent abroad, who is unfit to live in a community where the social glue holding it together is based on self-interest. He means for the best, is totally unselfish and nonegotistical, but ends up by bringing death, disaster and ruin upon those whom he loves, all the while aiding and abetting those who are his worst enemies. Montès is like a catalyst unleashing strong even violent reactions in other "elements" while he remains at the center of the drama seemingly untouched except for the tears silently falling down his unshaved cheeks. In the end, he is left alone, after the death of Rose, the departure of Maurice, and the adoption of the children by an unknown family. The last time he sees the girls is one of the most pathetic scenes in Simon's novels, second only to the departure of the narrator's wife in *Histoire* (see ch. 5). Montès is left with his memories of his stay in the unnamed town where he loved and lost; there is always the narrator whom he can talk to, but Montès appears to prefer to digest what has happened to him, to go over his memories. The world has shown itself to be one of disorder, "full of sound and fury," a "tale told by an idiot." There is no rhyme or reason, no how or why. All that remains is a disparate collection of unorganized memories of the past.

The other characters, though necessary to the drama

of *The Wind,* are not drawn in nearly as much detail as Montès: Rose, the chambermaid whose daughters Montès befriends; Jep, Rose's randy common-law husband; Maurice, a perpetual whiner who is staying in the same hotel as Montès; Cécile, Montès's rebellious cousin who symbolizes young womanhood; and Hélène, her practical, pragmatic and unemotional sister, who represents the matronly side of the female principle in Simonian terms.

The Wind can be considered as a kind of thematic reservoir, for Simon will again use many of its themes in later novels, such as the omnipotent and destructive force of time, the fragmented and disjointed character of human perception of reality, and memory with its subjective distortions of chronology and events. A resumé of the novel makes it sound more like a piece of pulp fiction than an experiment in writing. But what makes *The Wind* different from a dime-store novel is the thematization and problematization of storytelling within the very story that the narrator assembles from the bits and pieces he gleans from the principal actors involved in the drama. What Simon has done in this novel more overtly than in any other of his books is to demonstrate quite explicity just how difficult—even impossible—it is, not only to tell a story, but even to perceive fundamental reality. Characters' perceptions are inaccurate and at the best partial; memory plays havoc with the past, all of which is subject to the limits and restraints of language. While language in Simon is less than the ideal means of communication, it is also much more, since it can and obviously does acquire a momentum and a rhythm of its own which are independent of outside reality. All of Simon's *oeuvre* from *The Wind* to *The Georgics* (1981) is concerned with demonstrating through various means the quasi autonomy of language, its capacity for *creating* rather than just expressing meaning.[5]

The narrator must piece together Montès's story from what the latter tells him, and Montès's memory is far from photographic despite his interest in photos and engravings. Furthermore, Montès experiences reality as a series of disconnected episodes that do not necessarily happen in chronological order. And yet, due to the linear and sequential nature of language, the narrator must give his text a certain order, even though the material on which it is based presents itself as pure disorder. Storytelling therefore can only be a kind of compromise between two extremes. Hence the epigraph from the poet and essayist Paul Valéry (1871–1946) which Simon chose for his novel: "The world is incessantly threatened by two dangers: order and disorder." Storytelling is thematicized as a task as complicated as putting back together the pieces of a broken mirror.

[. . .] and now, now that it's all over, trying to report, to reconstitute what happened is a little like trying to stick together the scattered, incomplete debris of a broken mirror, clumsily struggling to readjust the pieces, getting only an incoherent, ridiculous, idiotic result; or perhaps only our mind or rather our pride forces us to risk madness and run counter to all the evidence just to find at any price a logical relation of cause to effect in the very world where everything the reason manages to make out is fugitive and vague [. . .]. (10–11, 10)

The resulting narrative is "idiotic" and "incoherent"; furthermore, it can only be "false, artificial, as any account of events is bound to be false after the fact" (51, 49). Now while the narrator is ostensibly speaking of Montès's story, Simon is, of course, giving us his version of storytelling, or better, of *story-writing,* which takes the form of a challenge thrown up in the face of conventional narrative and the assumptions upon which it is based.

In terms of structure, the novel consists of 17 chapters, varying in length from 24 pages to 3. In subsequent novels Simon never again made use of so many chapters. Given the thematic importance of fragmentation in *The Wind,* it is possible to understand why the author chose such a choppy form. On the other hand, the many chapters of the novel can be grouped into larger units or parts which, although not indicated as such, will become clear to the reader. Chapters 1–3 form the first part, presenting the main characters and the setting of the drama to be played out. As such, they fulfill the function of a dramatic exposition. Chapters 4–6 consitute the second part, fleshing out more elements in the story, for example, Rose and her little family. Chapters 7–9 form a third part. It is at the beginning of chapter 7 that the narrating "I" introduces himself. Chapters 10–13 form the fourth part with its dual climax: Hélène thwarts Maurice's attempts to blackmail her father, and Montès discovers the murder-suicide of Rose and Jep. Chapters 14–17 form the last part of the novel, a kind of resolution resolving nothing, since Montès loses access to Rose's children, not to mention his property. The tragedy is complete. In a novel which contains several allusions to baroque theater, it is not surprising that the drama played out is in five "acts." It should also be remembered that a baroque altar-piece with its three main panels plus the two outside or back panels would contain five parts as well. Thus, although the novel appears to have a rather loose structure, in fact it is highly structured.

From the point of view of technique, *The Wind* gives the reader a foretaste of Simon's writing in the 1960s by its extensive use of present participles, parentheses, ambiguous pronoun references, and the repetition of certain scenes (e.g. the narrator talking to Montès, to the notary) and leitmotifs (the fragmented nature of the characters' perception of reality). The wind is the most important of these recurrent leitmotifs and functions as a materialization of the passage of time. In its stubborn and destructive force, the wind seems to be part of a gigantic plot to destroy Montès, his plans and those he loves: "the long moan of the wind in the pines like the sound of exhausted, harassed time itself" (36–37, 35); "[the wind] intoxicated with its own rage, its own useless power" (43, 41). In the end, the sound of the howling wind is personified as a kind of complaint—one thinks of the notary's complaints at the outset of the novel as well as the whining, complaining voice of Maurice. "[. . .] wailing its long nightly complaint as if it were sorry for itself, envying the sleeping men, transitory and perishable creatures, envying them their possibility of forgetfulness, of peace: the privilege of dying" (254, 241). Here the wind could be said to anticipate the next of the author's novels in which the theme of death will play an important role. Even though *The Grass* does not recycle the characters of the 1957 novel, in terms of theme and technique, it represents a logical development in Simon's career as a novelist. As for readers of Simon, by the time they have completed working on *The Wind,* their rewarding though sometimes arduous apprenticeship as restorers of "baroque altar-pieces" is well underway.

NOTES

1. Alain Robbe-Grillet, *Pour un nouveau roman* (Paris: Minuit, 1963). Jean Ricardou's three books of criticism are highly technical: *Problèmes du nouveau roman* (Paris: Minuit, 1967), *Pour une théorie du nouveau roman* (Paris: Minuit, 1971) and *Le Nouveau Roman* (Paris: Seuil, 1973). More interesting to the general reader is *Three Decades of the French New Novel,* ed. Oppenheim.

2. See Claude Simon's untitled paper in *Three Decades of the French New Novel,* p. 73. Simon collaborated with Joan Miró on an art book entitled *Femmes* (Paris: Maeght, 1966). Furthermore, Simon's *Orion aveugle* (Blind Orion) (Geneva: Skira, 1970) contains reproductions of works of art as well as a text which he was later to recycle in his 1971 novel *Conducting Bodies.*

3. *The Wind,* trans. Richard Howard (New York: Braziller, 1959), p. 112; *Le Vent* (Paris: Minuit, 1957), p. 107. All subsequent references will appear in parentheses in the text.

4. Cf. Loubère, *The Novels of Claude Simon,* p. 63. Montès is modeled after Prince Myshkin.

5. It is for these reasons that *The Wind* is a good point of departure for the reader embarking upon a journey through the multifarious textual landscapes of Simon's fiction, since this early novel can be read as an "illustration and defense" of the author's aesthetic principles, his code of writing. In reading Simon's fiction it becomes clear that each of the novels fulfills a pedagogical function by teaching the reader how best to "decode" it. *The Wind* can be considered as the first step or lesson in the Simonian "syllabus."

CHAPTER TWO

The Grass
(*L'Herbe*)

Published in 1958, *L'Herbe* is the first in a series of five novels that make up Simon's second manner. Published over an 11-year period, the so-called Reixach Cycle owes its unity to the reappearance of related characters in different novels, as well as a certain similarity of style and technique, particularly an abundance of long sentences, parentheses, and present participles.[1] This is not to say that the novelist's style did not evolve over these years. On the contrary, in many ways the Reixach Cycle corresponds to the key period in Simon's career as a novelist precisely because it takes him and his readers from the early days of the second manner or stage of his writing to the more experimental texts of the third period characterized by *Triptych* (1973).

Different as Balzac and Simon are, there is a case to be made that Simon is France's Balzac of the twentieth century, for both writers use the technique of the novel cycle as well as long descriptive passages. While each of the texts in Simon's novel cycle is a whole and complete novel that stands by itself, it is nevertheless true that readers who have already read *The Grass* will bring to their reading of *The Flanders Road* background knowledge of some of the characters as well as familiarity with Simon's writing techniques, knowledge that can enhance their enjoyment of the later novel.

The story told in *The Grass* (which is set in 1952) comes after that of the 1960 novel, *The Flanders Road,* most of which takes place before, during and shortly after World War II. In *The Grass,* the story is centered on Louise and Marie, her husband Georges's maiden aunt, whereas in *The Flanders Road,* the story is centered on Georges's experiences before he married Louise. Since Simon's novels tend to grow out of each other and since each one represents a distinct attempt to come to grips with problems of narrative, they are best understood when read in the order in which they were originally published in French. Given the theme of the pursuit of knowledge, the reader of Simon soon becomes accustomed to this constant, relentless delving into different characters' pasts as the Simonian narrators seek to restore ever more complex Baroque altarpieces, to quote the eloquently descriptive subtitle of *The Wind.*

The Grass is told in the third person but adopts the point of view of one of the characters, Louise. It is the only one of Simon's novels to be narrated from the perspective of a female character. In fact, the novel is largely about three women: Louise, Sabine (her mother-in-law), and Marie (the latter's sister-in-law). The story is centered around a 10-day period in the summer of 1952 during which Marie is dying at age 84. The juxtaposition of actual perceptions, memories, and imagined scenes allows the narrative to play back and forth across the span of Marie's life. Through Louise's eyes, we see Marie now as a young career woman—she was a school teacher, one of the few careers open to women in the nineteenth century—now attending the marriage of her younger brother whom, along with her elder sister, Eugénie, she raised; now crossing half of the country at the time of the French debacle in June 1940 when she left her native Jura to travel to the southwest of France (near Pau) in order to be with her brother and his family. There is nothing sentimental about the way Marie's story is told, even though an old photograph leads Louise to speculate that Marie gave up love and marriage in order to raise her brother. Rather, Marie is presented as a hardnosed, practical woman equally at home in the classroom wielding a piece of chalk or digging in the vineyard of the family property. The men pale in comparison with the stronger female characters.

Like *The Wind,* the title of *The Grass* is nonanthropomorphic, referring to an element of nature to which we usually pay little attention. However, the title also contains a deep inlay of literary and artistic allusions. First, the title of Simon's novel harks back to a line of poetry by the nineteenth-century novelist, dramatist, and poet, Victor Hugo (1802–85): "Il faut que l'herbe pousse et que les enfants meurent" (The grass must grow and children must die).[2] Given that the principal character of the novel retains a childlike innocence and that *The Grass* recounts her dying, seen as a part of the natural cycle whereby all organic matter eventually returns to the earth, there is a clear relationship between this famous line about fatalistically accepting death and Simon's novel. Also, Hugo's second given name was Marie, the name of the dying woman. At the same time, the title of the novel also comes from a

31

passage by Boris Pasternak (1890–1960) chosen by Simon as an epigraph. It is taken from *Doctor Zhivago,* published just a year before *The Grass:* "No one makes history, no one sees it happen, no one sees the grass grow." History, as the novel will demonstrate, is not the stuff of textbooks, of dates and facts, but rather the day-to-day existence of ordinary people caught up in the web of life. It is interesting to note that in French, impersonal "history" and one's own personal "story" are one and the same word, *histoire.* There is also an allusion to the famous painting by Edouard Manet (1832–83), *Le Déjeuner sur l'herbe* (Luncheon on the Grass, 1862), which created a scandal in nineteenth-century France and which is still considered to be an important milestone in European art for its technique. Pictorial effects abound in *The Grass,* so that it is not surprising that the title should refer to this painting even though it is not referred to directly within the body of the novel. On the other hand, like the female nude in Manet's work, Louise is seen lying naked on the grass.[3]

The novel opens thus:

"But she has nothing, nobody, and no one will mourn for her (and what's death without tears?) except maybe her brother, and he's an old man now, and probably no more than she would mourn herself, I mean would allow herself to mourn herself, decide it was decent, was suitable to ..."

"But she's not related to you, why do ..."

"No," Louise said.[4]

From the outset, dying, death, and mourning are the subject, all of which seem final, definitive enough. But this is only part of the picture, for there is also a great deal that is in doubt: Who is speaking? And to whom? Who is dying? Why would the dying woman consider it indecent to cry? At the beginning of a first reading of *The Grass,* one does not understand, does not "see" the story, to use Pasternak's term. Of course, this is not through some fault or mistake on Simon's part, for the obscurity is programmed into the text: (hi)story defies seeing and perhaps the telling too. Only later will things gradually become clearer. For now, the emphasis is definitely on negation: *nothing, nobody, no one*, and *no more*; *nothing* and *no* are also repeated in the sentences that follow the ones quoted above. To underscore nothingness in such a way is entirely appropriate given the subject matter (death, dying), as well as the fact that we are dealing with a text that begins ex nihilo, out of nothing. Interestingly enough, "nothing" is also the second to last word of the narrative. It is a textual equivalent of the traditional formula used at Christian burials, "ashes to ashes, dust to dust."[5] However, by the time the reader has read the lines quoted, the picture already has become somewhat clearer—like a photo being developed before our eyes—since one may presume that in the initial dialogue the first sentence is spoken by the character Louise. What we do not know at this point is that she is talking to her lover (who will remain nameless and hidden in the darkness throughout the novel) and that the stoic whom they are talking about is Marie. It is because Louise is only related to the dying woman by marriage that the lover presumes that Marie is "nothing" to Louise, an opinion with which Louise disagrees totally. What then is Marie to Louise? The answer to

33

this question—the problematical relationship of an old lady who is dying in an upstairs bedroom to the younger, vital woman, who is lying in the grass with her lover—will determine both of their destinies, the lover's and Louise's. All the questions asked by such a problematic opening have the effect of luring us to read on, to attempt to solve the puzzle that the novel sets before us, in terms of character, theme, and technique.

The following family tree illustrates graphically the family relationships of the main characters. It will also be useful in reading *The Flanders Road* where several of the same characters recur.

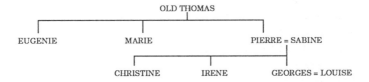

The daughter of an illiterate farmer, Marie-Arthémise-Léonie Thomas raised her brother with the help of her sister, who was also a school teacher. Fifteen years younger than his sister, Pierre is Marie's most obvious and biggest "creation." Always dressed plainly, she is fundamentally an innocent, a virgin whose wizened and dying body remains that of a child. (In Simon, children, virgins, and women are endowed with an uncanny otherworldliness that makes them unfathomable, like extraterrestrials.) During her long life, Marie refuses even to entertain the possibility of the existence of God or any kind of afterlife, preferring to admire the beauty of two passing butterflies when her sister-in-law pushes her on the subject. Her name is appropriate, for she is truly a doubting (Thomas) virgin (Marie).[6] Now lying on her future deathbed, unable to speak, Marie is near the end of the road: the sound of her death rattle, which goes on for the entire length of the novel, pervades every room of the big old house that already entombs her: "the old woman was dying, motionless in her solitary bed, the sheet which was drawn up to her chin rising and falling with the regular rhythm of that continuous, calm and terrible rattle escaping from her lungs" (17–18, 19). Two or three days after her stroke, the dying woman regains consciousness long enough to have an old box given to Louise. The box contains odds and ends, pieces of cheap jewelry, notebooks in which Marie wrote her household accounts, and, in one of these notebooks, a photo taken in 1896 in which she appears next to a gentleman caller who, Louise speculates, might well have been a suitor. These seemingly worthless pieces of "junk" are Marie's bequest to Louise.

While Louise forms the central narrative focus of the novel, it is not told in the first person. Her role is similar to that of a camera which allows us to see a series of cinematographic images, which does not mean that there is no subjectivity involved, for virtually everything is seen and felt from the young woman's point of view. Louise has been married to Georges, Marie's nephew, for about five years; she is currently having an affair with an engineer who is about to be transferred to Pau. Although her marriage to Georges is at an end, she is reluctant to leave the old house because of Marie, a woman who never asked anything of anyone, who gave what she could and even what she couldn't. The significance of Marie's gift to Louise is that it reinforces the feelings Louise already has for her husband's aunt. What we are dealing with is a unique form of nonverbal communication between two women who, despite their difference in age, still share much. If Marie finds the strength and the will to indicate to the attending nurse that Louise is to be given the box containing her life's "savings," then it must be because even in her agony she realizes that Louise alone will understand and appreciate them for what they are. Neither Marie nor Louise went off to war the way Georges did, so that their story is not "historic" in the usual sense of the word. Nor did Marie, who taught others to write, ever allow herself to write even a diary in which she could have expressed herself creatively. For example, one of the most traumatic events of her life—the onset of her sister's fatal illness—was noted down by Marie in her book of accounts simply by entering Eugénie's name (twice underlined). While Pierre was raised up by his two sisters to the status of university professor, they were content with their more humble station where everyone expected them to be happy and content. Of course, we are dealing with sexual stereotyping of an acute kind. Although it is unlikely that Marie would want Louise to imitate her and the life she led, one can appreciate the grandeur and the beauty of Marie's bequest. Those few trinkets and the notebooks symbolize not just the self-imposed abnegation which characterized Marie's calm existence, but also the passage of time itself during the 84 years of her apparently uneventful life. In Simonian terms, they are the true stuff of history, "not tragedy, screams, the accidental, the spectacular, but what constitutes, so to speak, the very warp of existence" (103, 123). Having received Marie's gift, Louise cannot leave, not because she still loves Georges or the family as such, but because she is now directly linked to a dying woman and her story. Thus *The Grass* can be viewed as a reformulation of what has traditionally been thought to constitute history; by writing this novel, Simon has provided the reader with an eloquent example of what should in all rights be called "her-story."

Georges, the son of Pierre and Sabine, originally followed in his father's and his aunts' footsteps, setting out to be a teacher before he failed his exams at the prestigious Ecole Normale Supérieure in Paris. Afterward, he "returned" to the earth, like his paternal grandfather, the illiterate farmer whose only ambition was to see his children educated. However, now Georges has nothing but contempt for his father's love of the written word. For Georges, books are as "lacking in reality and consistency as the air, the light" (123, 147). He is currently attempting to make a living out of a 10-acre orchard of pear trees which he bought with the money Marie gave him after the sale of the family property in the Jura. The operation is an agricultural and financial disaster as the fruit falls to the ground before it is ripe. The smell of rotting pears is the olfactory background to the action of the novel, just as Marie's belabored breathing is the acoustic background.

Sabine, one of the most clownlike of Simon's characters, would be truly tragic if she were not so pathetic. She is terrified of dying, unable to come to terms with the passage of time, hence the bright colors, the jewelry, the dyed hair, and the alcohol. As hysterical as Marie is stoic and calm, Sabine is a perpetual complainer. She never seems to stop talking, although no one really listens to her any more. She is especially indignant that Marie will not get a Christian burial as she (Sabine) thinks proper, that Georges may have taken one of her jewels to pay his gambling debts, and that her husband does not want to sleep in the same room as she. She is obsessed with sex and the many extramarital affairs that she presumes Pierre has had over the years of their marriage, going right back to the day of their wedding which took place fittingly enough in the year of a natural disaster in France: the great flood of 1910. Although not as old as Pierre or Marie—she is about 60 at the time of Marie's illness—in many ways Sabine seems to be the oldest person in the family precisely because she seeks to remain forever young by wearing loud jewelry and makeup. If the portrait painted of Sabine is so negative, she acts as a fitting foil to Marie.

Death, time, and history are significant themes in *The Grass*. As in *The Wind,* the problematic nature of reality is also of prime importance. Often language itself becomes the chief culprit, especially the supposedly rational and coherent use that young French men and women are taught to make of it, since "after all it's silly, it's even completely ridiculous to be forced, to think you're forced to express yourself coherently when what you're feeling is incoherent" (171, 207). Language as it is traditionally taught in school is perceived by Louise to deform both reality and our perception of it so that one ends up by understanding neither the "logic" of books nor "incoherent" reality:

> [. . .] the characteristic property of reality is to seem unreal, incoherent to us, since it presents itself as a perpetual challenge to logic, to common sense, at least as we have grown accustomed to see them predominate in books—because of the way in which words are arranged, the graphic or sonorous symbols of things, of sentiments, of excessive passions—, so that of course it sometimes happens that we ask which of these two realities is the real one. (84–85, 99–100)

Such a denunciation of books may surprise in an author who is so "literary." What should be remembered is that Simon is holding up to ridicule a certain use of language, as exemplified in *The Grass* by Pierre's scholarly research, in other words, institutionalized, learned expository discourse as it is taught and perpetuated in schools and universities, not just in France but everywhere in the modern world. In opposition stands a kind of primary, fundamental, "crude" use of language which is shown to be in harmony with basic human needs and drives. In *The Grass* such essential language takes the form of words inscribed on an ancient Roman monument. Now it is certainly not by chance that in a novel in which so many of the characters are teachers the model held up is a Latin text, for the language was widely taught in French schools. On the other hand, in Simon's novelistic universe Latin functions as a kind of wild or savage language that paradoxically has more in common with the illiterate peasant who tilled his land in the Jura than his learned son who, in the calm repose of his summer-house with its panes of colored glass, studies words and the history of their births and deaths. The use of language as a mere tool, that is, in a way that sets out to describe illogical feelings and urges in a supposedly logical manner, is thematicized as a debased, debilitating, and ridiculous enterprise. And just as *The Grass* can be read as "her-story," so too can it be read as a modern rewriting of those Latin words

> [...] which are not raw and improper but, apparently, specially conceived and created for bronze, the cemented stones of triumphal arches, aqueducts, monuments, the rows of words themselves cemented together, themselves like indestructible walls destined to outlast time itself, with the compact succession of their letters cut into corners, cubes, rafters, evenly spaced, arranged without punctuation, in capitals, without the slightest gap, like those walls constructed without mortar, the words controlling one another, ordered too by that imperious syntax [...] (108–09, 129–30). [Translation altered]

Unlike the previous novel, the text of *The Grass* is not broken up into any divisions other than paragraphs. In general, the structure of the 1958 novel is far more solid than that of *The Wind*. This is due in large part to the many motifs that recur regularly throughout the narrative: the sound of the rain, the smell of the rotting pears, the movements of the cat in the garden, and the sight and sound of a commuter train. Other recurrent motifs that add unity and texture to the novel are the T-shaped beam of sunlight

40

that passes through the shutters of the bedroom where
Marie lies dying and, of course, the many passages
which describe the tall grass where Louise and her
lover meet, for example "the thick wild grass silhouetted like brush-strokes of Chinese ink against the fad-
ing sky" (209–10, 254). Two other significant motifs are
the notebooks which Marie has the nurse give to Louise and the cookie box containing them. On the cover
of the box is a picture of a young woman wearing a
long white dress, lying on the grass, while in her hand
she holds a similar box on which is shown a similar
picture, and so on "like a series of mirrors without
end" (p. 11 of French edition, not translated in the
American edition). Now this pictorial rendition of an
infinite series functions in *The Grass* as an image of
the many repetitions and textual doublings which occur throughout the novel. As such it constitutes an
example of literary self-reflexivity which French critics call *mise en abyme:*[7] "the idea of this endless repetition which escaped the senses, the sight, precipitating
the mind into a kind of dizzying anguish" (153, 185).
This is not the only example of such a textual mirror
in Simon's works, but it is surely the most significant
for it functions as a canonic example of all the others
which the writer has included in his novels.

Despite the luxuriance of detail of plot and character, *The Grass* is not, any more than any other of Simon's works since the mid 1950s, a traditional novel.
Rather, the true emphasis of the novel is on the telling,
the *writing,* of the story. Images lead to new images,
comparisons engender comparisons and words generate other words as layer upon layer of intricate verbal
detail is built one upon another. Sometimes it becomes

difficult to follow the all-important parenthetical comments, but, unlike some modern writers, Simon does in fact close his parentheses. And despite the blurring of such significant details as dates and places, the narrative holds together. However, the reader will frequently have the experience of doing a double take. For example, it is easy (at least at first) to confuse the property in the Jura, where Eugénie and Marie brought up Pierre, with the house in the south, where Marie suddenly appeared in 1940 and where she is dying at the time of the narration; or the various days of the 10-day period while Marie lies dying (we never actually see her die); or even an epic argument between a drunken Sabine and her husband who is virtually crippled with fat and a scene preceding and immediately following one where Louise and her companion make love. The transitions from one scene to another are usually implicit; they are not underscored either by punctuation or other typographical devices. Hence the double takes which reproduce in narrative terms the cinematographic technique of fade-ins and fade-outs. For example, during the long argument between Sabine and Pierre, which Louise hears through the thin walls of the adjoining bathrooms, she imagines other scenes which are generated or triggered by certain key words. In one case, for example, the rain conjures up the image of an old grainy film (in which rain appears to be falling in front of the camera): "[. . .] glimpsed rather than seen through the scratches on the frayed reel [with] a little more of that surreality, of that inhumanity characteristic of creatures of the theater and of passion [. . .]" (159, 192). Louise then visualizes Pierre and Sabine as actors in a silent movie

42

of the 1920s. A typical Simonian technique consists of using a picture as a transition between two narrative sequences, either by animating a still or by immobilizing a "live" scene. In the case of the fight between Sabine and Pierre, they are transformed into a painting hanging in a picture gallery (186–87, 226–27), while the old photograph discovered in Marie's notebooks allows Louise to imagine what happened before and after the photo was taken (188–93, 228–34). Such transitions are often hidden in the text, and the reader must be alert to discover them so as to follow the narrative as it changes direction. Two scenes may flow into one another so subtly that the textual transition is almost invisible, like a fine joint in an exquisitely made piece of furniture. It should be clear that those passages that initially may make *The Grass* difficult to read are in fact very effectively written, for they are the most *evocative* (in terms of textual associations and echoes), as well as the most *provocative* (in terms of Simon's challenge to conventional narrative).

NOTES

1. The novels of Simon's second manner which make up the Reixach Cycle are as follows (dates refer to original French eds.): *The Grass* (*L'Herbe,* 1958), *The Flanders Road* (*La Route des Flandres,* 1960), *The Palace* (*Le Palace,* 1962), *Histoire* (1967, same title in English), *The Battle of Pharsalus* (*La Bataille de Pharsale,* 1969).

2. "A Villequier" in the collection *Les Contemplations,* 1856.

3. The allusions to Hugo and Manet are themselves contained in another reference which Simon no doubt had in mind when he chose the title of his novel, namely a passage from *Remembrance of Things Past* in which Marcel Proust (1871–1922) makes the following comment on Hugo's famous line: "To me it seems more correct to say

that the cruel law of art is that people die and we ourselves die after exhausting every form of suffering, so that over our heads may grow the grass not of oblivion but of eternal life, the vigorous and luxuriant growth of a true work of art, and so that thither, gaily and without a thought for those who are sleeping beneath them, future generations may come to enjoy their *déjeuner sur l'herbe*" (trans. C. K. Scott Moncrieff, and Terrence Kilmartin, and Andreas Mayor [New York: Vintage Books, 1981], vol. 3, p. 1095).

4. *The Grass,* trans. Richard Howard (New York: Braziller, 1960), pp. 9–10; *L'Herbe* (Paris: Minuit, 1958), p. 9. Subsequent references will appear in the text.

5. On the use and meaning of "nothing" in *The Grass,* see Stuart Sykes, *Les Romans de Claude Simon* (Paris: Minuit, 1979), pp. 47–48. One remembers that Flaubert dreamed of writing a book on "nothing," a dream which Simon has realized here.

6. As such Marie forms an ironic contrast with another famous aunt in French literature whose name she shares, the pious hypochondriac, Aunt Léonie, in Proust's *Remembrance of Things Past.*

7. Cf. Lucien Dällenbach, *Le Récit spéculaire. Essai sur la mise en abyme* (Paris: Seuil, 1977). Pages 171–73 are devoted to *The Grass.* The term *mise en abyme* is difficult to translate; the process involves the representation within the confines of an actual literary work of the writing, the reading, the plot outline, or even the formal structure of the text itself. The process is allegorical since such "secondary" meaning is superimposed upon the "primary" meaning, the story told by a novel. Actual examples of the technique can be thought of as mirrors or scale models.

CHAPTER THREE

The Flanders Road
(*La Route des Flandres*)

"I thought I was learning how to live, I was learning how to die." So Simon chose to begin *La Route des Flandres* (1960) by quoting Leonardo da Vinci in the epigraph to the first part of the novel. As in *The Grass,* one of the principal themes of the second in the five-novel Reixach Cycle is death. But unlike the previous novel, this one does not portray the slow peaceful death of an old woman who had sacrificed her life for others, but more violent kinds of death, including death on the battlefield, and, not coincidently, what the French call little death: sexual pleasure.

Claude Simon won the Prix de *L'Express* for *The Flanders Road,* his first literary prize in a career which would lead to the Nobel in 1985. Along with his later novels, *Histoire* (1967) and *The Georgics* (1981), the 1960 novel is one of Simon's longest and most famous works. The novel tells the story of the rout of French forces in World War II in the spring of 1940 after that period of the conflict known as the Phoney War. On the western front in continental Europe, the real war began with the German invasion of Belgium and France in May 1940, the blitzkrieg or lightning war. The novel is based on fact, since the French high command did indeed use the horse cavalry to oppose

German armored tank divisions and also the Luft-waffe.[1] The French army was defeated, and Claude Si-mon—like one of the principal characters of the novel, Georges, the future husband of Louise in *The Grass*—was sent to a POW camp in Nazi Germany. Simon had written of trying to oppose heavy artillery and bomber attacks with horses and rifles, especially in his early autobiographical work *La Corde raide* (1947), but *The Flanders Road* is the first novel he wrote about World War II. He returned to the subject in later novels, espe-cially *The Battle of Pharsalus, The World About Us,* and *The Georgics*. His 1960 novel constitutes a fitting and poignant memorial to his experiences during that conflict, and more important, to one man's attempts to come to terms with that past at a later time. In fact, the novel is more about the impossibility of knowing—the past, another person, even events to which one has been witness—than about war per se, which here is the fictional, though all important, "pretext" to the narra-tive.

The Flanders Road brings on stage several of the characters whom the reader of *The Grass* will recog-nize, not just Georges but also his parents, Pierre and Sabine; even Marie and Eugénie are mentioned in the later novel. In fact, the stories told in *The Grass* and *The Flanders Road* are so closely entwined that one could consider the latter as a kind of extended narra-tive parenthesis that has found a home of its own in separate covers. Aside from the recurring characters, there are also thematic concerns common to the two novels, for instance, the themes of time and history, and even certain leitmotifs such as the grass. This is not to say that the second novel of the Reixach Cycle simply rewrites the first. *The Flanders Road* is a longer, more complex work told in both the first and the third persons. Furthermore, the narrative thread of the Reixach family and their eighteenth-century ancestors is woven into the adventures of Georges and his family in a way that was not developed in *The Grass.* While neither Louise nor Georges reappear as named characters in any subsequent novels, the aristocratic de Reixachs do. Indeed, a novel such as *Histoire,* and even parts of *The Battle of Pharsalus,* will be easier to understand if one has already read *The Flanders Road.*

The title refers to a country road in that part of France and Belgium called Flanders, a plain extending along the North Sea which has been the site of many European wars. However, the road in question also alludes to the road of life,[2] the roads that lead to war, not to mention the "road" of writing. In conventional narrative, this road is more or less linear and unidirectional, but in Simon it is far more likely to be characterized by curves and zigzags as the narrative loops back on itself, just like the wanderings of the soldiers on that fatal day in May 1940. A road also figures prominently in a well-known definition of the novel: According to Stendhal (1783–1842), "[A] novel is a mirror journeying down the high road" (*Scarlet and Black,* 1830). Simon, whose aesthetic is diametrically opposed to nineteenth-century realism, does however include just such a mirror at the end of *The Flanders Road* when he describes what the captain would have needed to see himself in time—"a mirror with several panels."[3] Of course, with such a mirror de Reixach would have seen multiple reflections of himself, as in a hall of mirrors. *The Flanders Road* creates exactly this effect as the narrative comes back again and again to certain key episodes. Not that any definitive answers surface, for in Simon the proverbial whole truth remains an elusive even imaginary construct. Hence the working title of the novel which would have made a fitting subtitle, "Fragmentary Description of a Disaster."

The novel opens in the middle of a scene similar to a cinematographic closeup.

> He was holding a letter in his hand, he raised his eyes looked at me then the letter again then once more at me, behind him I could see the red mahogany ochre blurs of the horses being led to the watering trough, the mud was so deep you sank into it up to your ankles but I remember that during the night it had frozen suddenly [. . .]. (11, 9)

Given the hybrid nature of the sequence—part social scene, part sporting event—the reader could well think that the scene is set in a country house or at a horse show. However, as becomes obvious when one continues to read the first pages of the book, the scene quoted is neither of these. In fact the narrator has plucked it from his fund of memories of World War II, for the scene of the letter takes place at one of the overnight camps where Georges and his wartime buddies bivouacked during the winter of 1939–40. Now this is not to say that connotations of, on the one hand, high society and, on the other, the world of horse racing are absent from the story to be told. On the contrary, even the word "horse" (*cheval*) forms the kernel of a significant thematic cluster in *The Flanders Road*. As for the letter, it is a written reminder of social niceties, of an or-

48

dered world which predates the outbreak of war, like an odd souvenir from a foreign country: here from behind the front. A few lines below, we learn that it was written by the mother of "I" (i.e. Sabine in *The Grass*). Thus two men confront each other without speaking, as the letter literally comes between them. Ironically, it will turn out the purpose of the letter—to bring the two men (de Reixach and Georges) closer together— will be fulfilled in the end. What will bring these two cousins together is the death of the officer, de Reixach, and the attempts of the former private, Georges, to recreate through the powers of memory, imagination, and language the instant of and the reasons for the older man's death. If one considers the novel we are reading to be Georges's narration of this reconstitution, then *The Flanders Road* as a book, a space of *letters,* replaces and displaces the initial letter of the opening sequence.

The central enigma of the novel can be stated quite simply. During the French debacle of 1940, on a beautiful May afternoon, about 2 P.M. on a country road in Flanders, de Reixach, a captain in the French cavalry, is killed on horseback by a German sniper hidden behind a hedge. Long after the event the death of his cousin and commanding officer continues to fascinate Georges, who was present at the time as a soldier, because he thinks that de Reixach may have deliberately allowed himself to be killed. If so, his motivation is unclear. Was his death really a kind of suicide? Did he get himself killed because of the shame he felt due to the French defeat? Or was his "suicide" brought on by the shame he felt over his young wife's sexual infidelities? Descended from an eighteenth-century aristo-

49

cratic family, the captain has the appearance of a stiff, haughty representative of the French nobility as much out of place in the twentieth century, as he is in bed with a woman young enough to be his child. In many ways he is as much of an anachronism as the army's using the cavalry to repel German panzer divisions. It thus seems strangely appropriate that his last gesture—he raises his saber to defend himself against the fatal burst of machine gun fire—would be that of another age.

The Georges whom we meet in *The Flanders Road* is a younger incarnation of the character of the same name in *The Grass*. He too is somewhat of a contradiction. Although at age eighteen this son of a university professor already has nothing but sarcasm for the value of books and book learning, as another character points out, Pierre's son still talks like a book.[4] While Pierre deplores the loss to humanity represented by the bombing of the Leipzig library, Georges's position is that

[...] if the contents of the thousands of books in that irreplaceable library had been impotent to prevent things like the bombing which destroyed them from happening, I didn't really see what loss to humanity was represented by the disappearance of those thousands of books and papers obviously devoid of the slightest utility. (166, 224)

Georges thinks he prefers the world of real people and things to the abstractions of his father's "elegant phrases." He also thinks that he may learn something about the bizarre death of his enigmatic cousin by seeking out de Reixach's widow, the young and very beautiful Corinne. However, after the failure of their short affair, Georges wonders if his search for the truth (his cognitive and sexual quest) is really very different from his father's philological research. In both cases, an individual is attempting to discover or to reconstitute something to which he does not have direct access, the past. In both cases, all the (re)searcher can do is to speculate about what may or may not be the "truth"—if such a thing exists. But whereas Pierre's search is linguistic, Georges's is corporeal. What is more, in the end it is destructive of both Corinne and himself, since his quest culminates in a scene of sexual abuse.

> [. . .] thinking that after all she might have been right and that that wasn't the way, that is, with her or rather through her, that I will reach (but how can you tell?) perhaps it was as futile, as senseless as unreal as to make hen tracks on sheets of paper and to look for reality in words [. . .]. (218, 295)

Georges's three wartime buddies are Wack, Iglésia, and Blum. An anti-Semitic country bumpkin who prefers horses to people, Wack gets himself killed the day of the ambush. Iglésia is more developed as a character. A jockey of Spanish or Italian origin, he worked for de Reixach before the war, at which time he claims to have had a sexual relationship with his boss's wife. When war breaks out, he becomes de Reixach's orderly. Later he is interned in the same prisoner of war camp in Germany as Georges and Blum, where they get his story out of him fragment by fragment. What is not clear is whether he invents the story of his liaison with Corinne or whether it is the truth.

Blum is a young conscript of Jewish origin from the garment district of a large city, probably Paris. Despite or because of the differences in their backgrounds, Blum acts as Georges's double. In the camp they tell and retell each other real and/or imaginary stories about Corinne, de Reixach, and the eighteenth-century Reixachs to pass the time. It is not insignificant that apart from his dual role as "narratee"—the person to whom Georges narrates stories—and narrator, the other person who sometimes takes charge of the narration, Blum "represents" to a certain extent the Jews who died in the Holocaust. To be sure, Simon is not the kind of writer to discuss the political and historical issues of the twentieth century in general terms, for he is first and foremost a novelist, that is, a storyteller and poet. Nevertheless, it is certainly not by chance that he has included a Jewish character in *The Flanders Road*.[5] It is typical of Simon that he presents Blum without a trace of sentimentality, for Georges's soldier-companion is a sickly, cynical, street-smart complainer and whiner. Apart from Georges and the Reixachs, Blum is the most developed character of the novel. And what is more, when Blum disappears from the German POW camp—he probably dies from tuberculosis—Georges loses not only his best interlocutor and friend but also (and especially) part of himself, the Jew who is an integral part of each twentieth-century Everyman.

The three women characters play secondary roles. A girl with beautiful white skin is the object of the soldiers' erotic fantasies, particularly of Georges. Glimpsed at the farm where Georges, Blum, Wack, Iglésia, and de Reixach bivouac in the fall of 1939, she is the wife of a local farmer to whom she has apparently been unfaithful with the mayor's assistant. The story seems as difficult to piece together for Georges and his comrades as it is for us. More important from the point of view of thematics is the fact that such a fleeting glimpse of sensuality is part and parcel of the Simonian association of femininity with whiteness, light, and milk.[6] On the other hand, despite Sabine's continual attempts to constitute herself as subject (in her capacity as principal authority about the family tree), she succeeds only in becoming more and more of an object, a rather undignified one at that. Even language itself becomes reified in Sabine's mouth as she prattles on endlessly about the de Reixachs.

Corinne, the main female character of the novel, will reappear in *Histoire,* and briefly in *The Battle of Pharsalus* and *Triptych.* Like the unnamed girl with milky skin, Corinne is an object of sexual fantasies on the part of Blum and Georges who get Iglésia to tell them stories about de Reixach's young wife. After the war, she and Georges become lovers for some months. When Georges talks to Corinne about his wartime experiences, she feels that he is talking, not to her but rather through her to Blum, or just to himself. Unlike Sabine, she is never the subject of her own story—she is described almost entirely as a sexual object—until she leaves Georges because she feels abused by him and his passion which reduce her to a kind of sexual toy. She compares his feelings for her to the pornographic drawings found in the latrine of a soldiers' barracks! However, it should be noted that Corinne does rebel against Georges and that it is she who walks out on him, literally leaving him in the dark. Although we

53

never learn Corinne's story from her directly, by her gesture of refusal and revolt, she acts as subject, not of the narration but of the action of the story.[7]

Pierre does not differ from his role in *The Grass,* namely, that of an intellectual fat cat. Sitting in the summerhouse with its multicolored windowpanes, Georges's father literally sees the world through the equivalent of rose-colored glasses. He lives through and for the written word, something for which his son at first has little use.

There is one other major character who, along with Wack, Blum and Captain de Reixach, is dead at the time of the narration: Georges's maternal great-great-great-grandfather, Henri Reixach. Despite his aristocratic origins, the eighteenth-century Reixach (who dropped the noble particle *de* from his name although his nineteenth-century descendants were later to restore it) was a soldier participant in the French Revolution, including the Convention (1792–95), and the revolutionary wars that ensued.[8] A great admirer of the Swiss born preromantic writer Jean-Jacques Rousseau (1712–78), whose complete works he possessed, Reixach is portrayed as a naïve idealist. When confronted by the less than ideal circumstances of real life, Reixach appears to have had resort to suicide.[9] However, as is the case with his twentieth-century namesake, the circumstances of the first Reixach's death are unclear. Did he commit suicide after discovering the infidelities of his beautiful wife, Virginie? Or was it because of the Spanish rout of the French army? Or perhaps out of disappointment with what had become of the original ideals of the Revolution? Did one of Virginie's lovers perhaps shoot him? Blum and Georges imagine different versions of the story that lead up to the rumored but scandalous "facts" about the discovery of Reixach's body, which was supposedly found naked in the very same room that was to become Georges's parents' bedroom many years later. In *The Flanders Road,* the political, military, and intellectual history of France mingles with family gossip and scandal, not to mention childhood fantasies and the need of the two teenagers to tell each other stories in order to forget their hunger or just to while away the time in a German POW camp. As a child, Georges was particularly fascinated by an old painting in his family's possession, a portrait of Reixach with a bleeding head "wound."

[. . .] that portrait which all during his childhood he had looked at with a kind of uneasiness, timidity, because he (that distant progenitor, sire) had in his forehead a red hole from which the blood ran down in a long undulating rivulet starting at the temple, following the curve of the cheek and dripping on to the lapel of the royal-blue hunting coat [. . .]. (46, 56)

In fact, the hole is not a pictorial representation of Reixach's suicide or murder since the painting had deteriorated considerably over the years and the redness is part of the original preparation of the canvas coming through the paint.[10] Of course, the portrait is all the more evocative and disturbing since neither Georges nor Blum (nor Simon) is content with realistic or pragmatic solutions to such a bizarre and fascinating historical puzzle. In reading *The Flanders Road,* the reader soon learns that the two Reixachs form mirror images of each other, not just because of the many similarities between them, but also because in both cases the stories told about them resist any and all attempts to discover and articulate the factual "truth." Thus, both Henri Reixach and Captain de Reixach are archetypal creatures of fiction.

Since the novel is not narrated chronologically, one must keep in mind the various "moments" or loci of the fiction which stretch roughly over a 150-year period, from the French Revolution to the immediate postwar period in France in the 1940s. Any ordering of the narrative into something ressembling a traditional plot should not diminish the originality of the novel whose significance hardly depends on a coherent story. On the other hand, if one can identify the various spatio-temporal scenes of the narrative, one can also appreciate the intricacy of the thematic and verbal weaving that has gone into the writing of the novel.

I. After returning to France from Spain, the eighteenth-century Reixach dies from a pistol shot.

II. In the decade preceding World War II, Corinne marries de Reixach; she may have had brief and impersonal sexual encounters with her husband's employee Iglésia. In a futile gesture to prove his manhood or riding ability (which here are one and the same thing) de Reixach insists one sultry June afternoon on replacing his jockey in a steeplechase which he loses.

III. 1939

    A. In "the stagnant heat of August, of the rotting summer" (31, 37), Pierre and Georges attempt to speak to each other shortly before Georges leaves for the army.

B. Georges and his fellow soldiers are billeted at a farm in the Ardennes region of northeastern France after a long ride in the night and the fall rain; Georges sees a young woman with luminescent white skin.

IV. 1940
   A. May 1940: The French retreat takes place during 10 days at the end of the month.
      1. On the fatal day at dawn, the regiment is ambushed and Georges's squadron is almost totally massacred; after the ambush Georges spends several hours lost in some woods.
      2. In the afternoon, Georges happens upon his squadron, now reduced to four men: de Reixach, the sublieutenant, de Reixach's orderly—Iglésia—and Georges himself.
      3. At about 2 o'clock in the afternoon, on a stretch of road in Flanders running almost due east-west, de Reixach and the sublieutenant are killed by a German sniper.
      4. Later on Georges and Iglésia attempt to flee wearing civilian clothes; they get drunk on gin in a village café.
   B. May 1940: After being captured by the Germans (a scene not described), Georges is forced to lie in a field along with other French prisoners of war.
   C. June (?) 1940: The prisoners are transported to Germany under terrible conditions in cat-

tle cars; at one point, the train stops and more prisoners are forced into the car, among them, Blum.

V. In the POW camp, Iglésia, Georges, and Blum spend their time telling tales of the past, "summoning up the iridescent and luminous images by means of the ephemeral, incantatory magic of language" (137, 184); at one point, Georges attempts to escape but is captured.

VI. After the end of the war, Georges looks up Corinne, and they have an affair that lasts for some months. Early one morning at the end of summer in 1946, after a night spent in a hotel room, she leaves, accusing him of not really loving her. It is the backdrop of this night's activities—the sex and the story-telling—that constitutes the narrative "present" of the novel.

The Flanders Road is as thematically rich as it is complex in terms of chronology. In fact, themes fulfill an important structural function since they provide the textual glue that gives the novel its overall unity. According to the critic Jean Ricardou, one such "super-theme" is that of disintegration, which paradoxically holds the entire novel together.[11] In a way it is a mis-nomer, since Simonian disintegration most often takes the form of a *mutation* of an existing order into a new one. During the crucial events in May the front disin-tegrates, the French army disintegrates, the regiment disintegrates, the squadron disintegrates: "[. . .] not war not the classical destruction or extermination of one of the two armies but rather the disappearance the absorption by the primal nothingness or the primal All

58

of what a week before were still regiments batteries squadrons of men [. . .]" (221, 299). Later on, the only ones left are two officers and two soldiers, before the former are killed. In the end, Georges's friendship with Blum comes to an end due to the deterioration of the latter's health and the visible disintegration of his body before he finally just disappears from the scene. As for Georges's postwar relationship with Corinne, it too is destined to disintegrate before his astonished eyes when she walks out on him. Physical disintegration is exemplified by the decomposition of the horse's body, which Georges sees several times on that fateful day in May when de Reixach is killed. Earlier on, during the night of the long ride in the fall of 1939, the whole countryside seems to be dissolving in the rain: "It had started raining again, or rather the landscape, the road, the orchard had begun to melt again, silently, slowly, decomposing, dissolving into a fine dust of water that slipped past without a sound [. . .]" (48, 59). As for human creations, even so-called cultural objects fare no better, for example, Reixach's portrait has been disintegrating for years. Physical and sexual death may emphasize and accelerate the process of decomposition, but it is already always universal and everlasting. Fittingly enough the novel ends with a description of the whole world subject to the overall disintegration brought on by the passage of time: "[. . .] the world stopped frozen crumbling collapsing gradually disintegrating in fragments like an abandoned building, unusable, left to the incoherent, casual, impersonal and destructive work of time" (231, 314).

Once again Simon incorporates into his novel the theme of knowledge, or perhaps it would be more accurate to say the theme of the impossibility of knowledge. Inextricably linked with Georges's affair with Corinne, as well as his father's scholarly research, it is also closely associated with the theme of order and disorder. Traditional history—the stuff of textbooks—takes the form of a falsely reassuring order imposed by us on brute reality, or rather, on our perception of reality, or rather, on our memory of perceived reality. So strong is our strange need to establish, to create, supposedly logical and causal relationships between various phenomena. "History (or if you prefer: stupidity, courage, pride, suffering) leaves behind it only a residue abusively confiscated, disinfected and finally made edible, for the use of official school textbooks and pedigreed families ... " (140, 188 [trans. alt.]). In Simon, it is impossible to attribute any definitive causes to events of personal or historical import—such as the death of Henri Reixach—for they have multiple causes, all of which seem equally plausible. Our eternal need to know facts for certain is seen to be an illusion, a trap which we set for ourselves, since there is simply no way of knowing things for certain. Which is not to say that Simon's characters do not seek to gain knowledge about the past, both the recent past to which they have been witness as well as the more remote past about which they have just heard. The questions "How could anyone tell?" and "How can you tell?" are like a musical refrain that comes back again and again throughout the novel; they underscore the desperation of Georges's search for the truth. As mentioned, his cognitive and sexual quests form a vivid contrast with his father's linguistic research, which Georges ends up viewing as no more futile than his own type of "research." As the critic David Carroll has pointed out, Simon does not favor either of these two quests for knowledge. "But it is not a question of choosing between the two positions, between absolute, naive optimism and gloomy, regressive nihilism, between Georges's argument against books and knowledge and that of his father, who gives them an absolute value. Rather the novel is constructed in terms of the conflict between the two positions, in terms of the inadequacy of either as a universal statement. The novel continually undercuts and situates all positions which pretend to be universal [...]."[12] The thematic significance of eroticism is great; it serves as a kind of textual link between the quest for knowledge and the quest for sexual pleasure. At first, eroticism in Simon appears to be very graphic and even crude, for sexual couplings are described in terms of basic biological urges and animal drives rather than as love.

> [...] so not much question of love, unless it just happens that love—or rather passion—is what it was: that wordless thing, those impulses, those repulsions, those hatreds, all unformulated—and even unformed—, and then that simple series of actions, words, insignificant scenes, and, at the centre, without preamble or preparation that assault, that urgent swift, fierce grapple, anywhere, maybe in the stable itself [...]. (42, 51)

But to say that the many descriptions of various types of sexual activities in *The Flanders Road* are pornographic is to miss the point. To appreciate fully the theme of eroticism it must be viewed in the overall context of the novel. It is true that there are many overt and explicit descriptions of Georges and Corinne engaging in various sexual practices (not to mention Iglésia and Corinne's rapid couplings). At the same time, a more general, all-pervasive eroticism is attached as "secondary" or connotative meaning to many if not all of the scenes that are not openly sexual, for example, the union of cavalryman and horse, even the mingling of bodies and entwined limbs in the cattle car, as well as the scenes where the French POWs lie on the ground, in intimate contact with the earth and the grass. Verbal allusions, chromatic harmonies, similes, metaphors, and even puns play the role of textual intermediators as the distinction between the erotic and the nonerotic is blurred more and more while the reader progresses through the novel until the textual climaxes of the third part are reached. It then becomes clear that what is the most erotic may not be what is the most explicit but what at first may seem ordinary. Eroticism in Simon involves not just the sexual or the nonsexual, but the passage or movement of the narrative from one domain to another as words and sequences couple with each other in a kind of textual and verbal orgy. This puts the emphasis squarely on the reading of the novel as a finely wrought cultural and literary artifact, the opposite of the usual purpose and effect of pornography. Clearly, Georges's conduct vis-à-vis Corinne is *phallocratic,* and the actual descriptions of sex acts are definitely *androcentrist.* However, in terms of the overall economy of the novel, eroticism as a theme has neither of these characteristics for it is truly organic and even *pantheistic,* literally involving all of nature.

As to structure, the three parts of the novel are of

unequal length, the longest being the central panel or chapter. The tripartite structure recalls the original subtitle of *The Wind* and will be used again by Simon in his 1973 novel, *Triptych*. The three parts of *The Flanders Road* do not correspond simply to three chronological divisions of the novel. The temporal loci of the story, just like the themes, tend to overlap and become entwined. However, such spatial patterning of the narrative is significant for it gives the novel an artistic structure of its own above and beyond the limits imposed by conventional chronology. The structure is roughly symmetrical since two of the most important episodes are narrated in the middle of the novel, the one embedded within the other: the horse race in which de Reixach insists upon replacing Iglésia as jockey on a June afternoon sometime before the war, and the destruction of the captain's squadron and his subsequent death on a May afternoon in 1940.

The narrative voice alternates throughout the novel. All told, about one-third of the novel is in the first person, the rest in the third person. The opening pages (to p. 27 in the original French edition and p. 24 in the English translation) and part 3 are symmetrical in their use of the first-person pronoun. The third person can be interpreted both as Blum, Georges's double, *and* as another impersonal part of Georges's consciousness.[13] The repeated shifts in narrative voice throughout the novel serve to remind the reader that for Simon the act of narration is not simple or straightforward but highly problematical. Furthermore, just as the identity of the narrator is not singular and certain, so too the identity of the person to whom the story is told is not clear either, for the so-called narratee is sometimes Georges's father, sometimes Blum, sometimes Corinne, and sometimes a part of Georges himself.

The text of *The Flanders Road* is highly repetitive. The first type of repetition involves the coming back of the narrative to a scene that only occurred once in "reality," for instance, the death of de Reixach which is approached several times before the final, "definitive" version at the end of part 3. This kind of recurrent scene illustrates Georges's fascination with the enigma that de Reixach's death represents for him. The second kind of repetition is that of an episode which actually does occur more than once in the story, for example, the various times that Georges sees the rapidly decaying body of a dead horse.[14] But repetition does not just involve actual content but also structure. No doubt the most abstract form of structure is one based on "mere" mathematics. In fact, *The Flanders Road* contains a multitude of symmetrical structures based on numbers. For example, there are two cafes, two sick or dead horses, two Reixachs who are military officers, two beautiful wives, two doubles (Georges and Blum); there are three suicides, three cuckolds, "three ghosts three grotesque and unreal shadows with their fleshless faces" (128, 172), three times when Georges lies in the dark; there are four riders who end the steeplechase, four horsemen on the Flanders road (reminding one of the four horsemen of the Apocalypse: Conquest, War, Famine, Death), four times that Georges sees the dead horse; there are five horses with de Reixach when he is shot, five defeats (the rout of the French army in Spain at the beginning of the nineteenth century, the end of the first Reixach's marriage, the military debacle of the French in 1940, the fiasco of the second Reixach's marriage, the end of Georges's liaison with Corinne). Of course, such a list is far from complete, but it is clear that in Simon structure is significant and even capable of creating meaning in and of itself. Not due to mere chance or the historic "truth," such symmetrical structures predetermine or generate each other, as in poetry and music.

As to technique, *The Flanders Road* makes even greater use of a device already employed in the earlier novels, particularly *The Grass:* narrative transitions from one spatial or temporal locale of the fiction to another. At first reading, this can be disconcerting, since readers may well miss the transition only to learn that they have deliberately been led down the proverbial garden path and that in fact the text is talking about something else. Hence the reflex of the double take, and not a little confusion and even frustration. For example, one continues to read a passage thinking that it is a wartime scene—the transport of the French POWs to Germany in cattlecars—when, almost after the fact, one realizes that it is a postwar scene involving a man and a woman who are passionately making love (cf. part 3). Now reader reaction to such abrupt and apparently hidden narrative transitions can be compared to two drinkers confronting their half full/half empty glasses. One can compare the pessimistic drinker to readers who demand that a novel tell them a real story. Upon realizing just how apparently fragmented the text is, these readers cry foul. They see only emptiness in terms of what they think a novel should be. On the other hand, readers who examine the text closely in order to determine the

65

exact location and the raison d'être of the transitions will become aware that the apparent breaks are in fact examples of narrative *continuity*. We are all familiar with similar experiences in seeing films and videos when one scene overlaps or fades into another. Repetition of a name, a word, a color, or even a partial verbal echo allows the text to change tracks, so to speak.

There is no better example of a transition than the following passage—supposedly taken from an eighteenth-century text—which describes a hybrid creature.

Everything in the Centaurefs is graceful and delicate and all deserves to be considered with an especiall attencion The node and juncture where the human part ends and the equine part begins is indeed admirable The eye distinguishes the delicacie of the white flesh-tintes in the woman from the clarity of the brilliant fur in the animal of a light chestnut colour but one is then confused in attempting to determine the confines. (45, 55–56)

This passage is one of the most important keys to an understanding of the novel since it thematicizes, in the form of the description of an engraving, a technique fundamental to Simon's writing, both at this stage of his career as well as later. In *The Flanders Road,* scenes, characters, and even centuries overlap each other so that it is often difficult to identify an episode or a textual fragment as belonging to one particular spatio-temporal locus of the fiction. In the passage quoted above, the technique of overlapping (*chevauchement* in French, from the word for "horse") is described fittingly enough in the form of a being

66

half-woman and half-horse. One thinks of Corinne, for to Georges and his buddies she seems as nonhuman as a filly (the word is properly ambiguous). While both parts of the engraving are said to be especially fine, it is impossible to determine exactly where the human part leaves off and the animal part begins. In other words, Simon is giving us a key to his vision of the world and his writing: in both, things, people, animals, events are not distinct, but rather end up overlapping, superimposing each other because of their fundamental similarities. The difference is not marked by a firm border, either in reality or in Simon's words.

To put the emphasis only on shifts in the story is to miss the point that a novel is first and foremost a *text,* a piece of writing, and that words and their connotations are just as important as the adventures of the characters. The goal is to become aware and, it is to be hoped, appreciative of a kind of writing which "bares the device," unmasks the ultimate fiction that would have us believe that we are dealing with real people and real situations and not a text. *The Flanders Road* is a novel about World War II, but it is also a novel in which the author has allowed himself to explore language and exploit its generative capacities. To read Simon well one has to *see* the ways in which he uses *words,* as much as imagine the scenes which are conjured up in the mind's eye. While readers of the original French version will have more opportunity to appreciate this kind of wordplay, Richard Howard's rendition of the text is brilliant, so that even in the English translation readers will have ample opportunity to appreciate *The Flanders Road* for what it is, a novel that has been crafted by a gifted writer.

NOTES

1. See Anthony Cheal Pugh, "Defeat, May 1940: Supplementary History. Before, and After, *La Route des Flandres*" in *The Second World War in Literature,* ed. Ian Higgins (Edinburgh: Scottish Academic P, 1986), pp. 121–30. Pugh quotes a two-page text by Simon in which the writer gives a bare bones outline of the events in which he was involved in 1940.

2. Dante's *Inferno* begins with the line, "Midway in the journey [road] of our life."

3. *The Flanders Road,* trans. Richard Howard (London: Calder, 1985 [1961]), p. 231; *La Route des Flandres* (Paris: Minuit, 1960), p. 313. Subsequent references will appear in the text.

4. One is reminded of Jean-Paul Sartre (1905–81), the famous French intellectual and man of letters who questioned the value of the traditional humanities and liberal arts.

5. Blum recalls another Jewish character in twentieth-century literature, Bloom in *Ulysses* (written 1914–21) by James Joyce (1882–1941).

6. On the mythic significance of this vision of femininity, see Karen Gould, *Claude Simon's Mythic Muse* (Columbia, S.C.: French Literature Publications, 1979), pp. 46–48, 52. On the details of the marital imbroglio, see Doris Kadish, *Practices of the New Novel in Claude Simon's "L'Herbe" and "La Route des Flandres"* (Fredericton, New Brunswick: York, 1979), p. 60 n.

7. On the subject of androcentrism, see Lynn A. Higgins, "Gender and War Narrative in *La Route des Flandres," L'Esprit créateur* 27.4 (1987): 17–26. See also Chapter 10.

8. In writing about Reixach's revolutionary activities, Simon seems to have had a primitive model of LSM in *Les Géorgiques* in mind, although they are not the same character.

9. For a comparison of Reixach's, Pierre's, and Rousseau's idealism, see David Carroll, *The Subject in Question: The Languages of Theory and the Strategies of Fiction* (Chicago: U of Chicago P, 1982), pp. 134–37.

10. A reproduction of the painting Simon had in mind when he wrote about the uncanny portrait of Georges's eighteenth-century ancestor is to be found on the front cover of the paperback French edition of *La Route des Flandres* (Paris: Minuit [collection "Double"],

1982), as well as in the volume of *Entretiens* devoted to Simon (Rodez: Subervie, 1972).

11. On the theme of disintegration, see Jean Ricardou, "Un ordre dans la débâcle" in *Problèmes du nouveau roman,* pp. 44–55.

12. Carroll, *The Subject in Question,* pp. 136–37.

13. According to Doris Kadish, "The *I* who speaks at the beginning and end of the novel, and intermittently in between, is a character who strives, but ultimately fails, to create his subjectivity through language. His failure can be seen in his repeated losses of that which is the sole constituent factor of his subjectivity, namely, his voice. Repeatedly *I* experiences the usurping of his subjectivity by *he*—that is, by himself as an impersonal object in his consciousness" (*Practices of the New Novel,* p. 70).

14. According to Simon himself, one can imagine the travels of the soldiers on that traumatic day in May 1940 taking the form of a cloverleaf, the point of intersection of the three loops indicating the position of the dead horse (cf. Hubert Juin, "Les secrets d'un romancier, *Les Lettres françaises*" [Oct. 6, 1960]: 5).

69

CHAPTER FOUR

The Palace
(*Le Palace*)

Le Palace, published in 1962, is one of five books written by Claude Simon in which the Spanish Civil War
(1936–39) plays an important part. He wrote about the
conflict that had such a great influence on twentieth-
century intellectuals in his early autobiographical
work, *La Corde raide* (The Tightrope, 1947) and in an
untranslated novel, *Le Sacre du printemps* (The Rite
of Spring, 1954). After the 1962 novel, he was to return
to that war in *Histoire* (1967) and again in *The Georgics*
(1981). Clearly the Spanish War and, in particular,
events that happened in Barcelona at that time constitute an important reservoir of memories, impressions,
and feelings for this French writer, who did indeed go
to Spain during the war.

While it is not necessary to know in detail the intri-
cacies of the complicated political situation in Spain
at the time of the civil war in order to appreciate *The
Palace,* some background knowledge may prove help-
ful. The conflict, a kind of horrible warm up for World
War II, ended in the defeat of the Spanish government
and the victory of the right-wing Falange Party led by
Generalissimo Francisco Franco (1892–1975) after a
bitter and bloody struggle between the Republican
Loyalists and the Nationalists. The progovernment

Loyalists received help from Russia and from members of the International Brigade, who came to the defense of the Spanish Republic from many countries around the world, including the United States (Abraham Lincoln Battalion), while the rebels received help from Fascist Italy and Nazi Germany. The Loyalist government based in Barcelona was made up of a coalition of various political parties and factions, including socialists, communists, Trotskyites, and anarchists. The situation in wartorn Barcelona, the last bastion before the city was taken by Franco's Nationalists in January 1939, was further complicated by a kind of local war within the larger conflict when the Spanish Left turned upon itself and members of various factions started to kill one another.[1] This internecine fight leading to the takeover of the Left by communists under orders from Moscow is treated fictionally in *The Georgics*.

The Palace is the third novel of the Reixach Cycle, although for readers who tackle the novels in the order in which they were published, the links of this text to the earlier ones will not become apparent until they read the next book in the cycle, *Histoire*. *The Palace* is the first novel of Simon's so-called second manner of writing in which he utilizes the thematic reservoir of the Spanish conflict, thus expanding the fictive universe of the cycle which had until then been limited to the adventures of Georges Thomas and those directly connected to him. *The Palace* is also Simon's only novel entirely devoted to the Spanish Civil War.[2] But given the author's tendency to question and challenge conventional storytelling techniques, his 1962 novel is no more a traditional war story than his next novel could be construed to be a traditional love story. In fact, while the war in Spain forms the fictional backdrop to the narrative, *The Palace* is as much about coming to terms with one's own past and one's former self; just as *The Flanders Road* was about attempts to reconstruct another's past. Here the past takes the form of the reworked memories of a participant, or rather an onlooker, in the civil war who, fifteen years after the events took place, visits an unnamed city where Spanish is spoken. As such, Simon's novel constitutes a new version, a rewriting, of stories about the Spanish conflict by older writers: *L'Espoir* (1937, *Man's Hope*) by André Malraux (1901–76), *Le Mur* (1939, *The Wall*) by Jean-Paul Sartre (1905–80), and *For Whom the Bell Tolls* (1940) by Ernest Hemingway (1898–1961). Among other things, Simon's 1962 novel provides an implicit denunciation of the lies of political rhetoric and the crimes done in the name of political expediency, even and especially when they are "for a good cause." Often it is not easy to digest *The Palace,* which should not be surprising since two of the principal motifs are indigestion and decay. All things considered, there appears to be a lot of rot—both physical and political—in the city described in *The Palace*. To a certain extent the novel is about the always painful loss of youthful ideals. More significant, it attempts, through the act and process of writing, to come to terms with past memories, feelings, and impressions, an enterprise made all the more difficult because of the fact that they overlap and superimpose themselves on each other. Hence the complexity of the writing, the painstaking detail of the descriptions, and the embedding of parentheses within parentheses.

The title refers to a palatial hotel, which is the meaning of the word in French. At the same time, *Le Palace* can be read as an almost perfect anagram of *la place* (the square). By its title one might be tempted to think that the novel will describe the lives of the rich and famous who can afford to stay in some grand hotel located on a famous square. In fact, the foreign tourists who once occupied the luxurious suites are conspicuous by their absence since the Palace has been requisitioned for office space by a beleaguered left-wing government. The title itself already contains an allusion to the executive and judicial branches of government in the form of a palace (Fr. *palais*) as well as a law courts building (Fr. *palais de justice*). Hence the images, on the one hand, of a queen left alone in a royal palace to die from a hemorrhage after giving birth to a deformed baby (ch. 5), and on the other, of quick justice and summary executions that take place in the night (ch. 3).

The novel's epigraph quotes a dictionary definition of the word "revolution": "the locus of a moving body which, describing a closed curve, successively passes through the same points." A revolution often refers to a complete break with the past, whether political, social, or economic. Simon has chosen to quote what would appear to be a nonpolitical definition of the term in order to remind the reader that the word also has a geometrical or astronomical meaning when used to describe a circular movement. One then wonders if the two meanings of the word are as distinct as might be imagined. For example, a revolution that led to as much political oppression as it sought to eliminate could be considered doubly or even intrinsically revolutionary. Finally, the title is directly linked to the epigraph, for a palace revolution is a top-echelon change in the power structure of an organization or government that does not have grass roots support. This already gives the reader an important clue to the political drama that forms the backdrop of the narrative. As for the dictionary quoted, it is named after a nineteenth-century educator and lexicographer, Pierre Larousse (1817–75). Geometry, astronomy, and political history—this series of subjects implicitly conjures up the image of a student (or an ex-student as the former revolutionary is called in *The Palace*) using a dictionary to help him understand his assignments, or just to help him write ... [3]

As with all Simon's novels, the opening lines are essential, and the rest of the text is inextricably linked to them.

> And all at once, in a sudden rush of air, immediately stilled (so that it was there—wings already folded back, perfectly motionless—without their having seen it, as if it hadn't flown to the balcony but had suddenly appeared there, materialized by a magician's wand), one of them landed on the stone balustrade, enormous (probably because you always see them from a distance), strangely ponderous (like a porcelain dove, he thought [. . .]).[4]

At first the reader is confronted with an immediate and startling impression—the rustling of air, feathers—before he is told the factual information that a bird has landed on the ledge of a balcony. The narrative starts in medias res, and once again we are immediately put off our guard. Then we realize that this is exactly the impression of those (for the moment un-known) persons who witness the arrival of the pigeon. Or rather, they don't see it arrive; it is just suddenly there. Like the beginning of the book just opened by the reader—white space followed by the onset of printed words on the page—so too the narrative begins by recounting the sudden appearance, the abrupt ma-terialization, of an as yet unknown entity. The first chapter of the novel is entitled "Inventory," a word with commercial connotations. However, an inventory is also a text, albeit a list, and like a text—or the sudden appearance of the pigeon—it must have a be-ginning, ex nihilo, out of nothingness.

It should be noted also that the pigeon arrives more than once in these first few lines of text, for the actual arrival of the bird ("one of them landed") is preceded by a parenthesis describing the manner in which the bird appears. One could even say that the bird arrives *three* times, for it is not until several lines further into the text that the word "dove" is mentioned. Just as the passage underscores the typical Simonian theme of the passage from movement to immobility, the passage also thematicizes the notion of strangeness: the bird is strangely heavy ... like a porcelain dove. Of course, a porcelain dove is an inanimate object made to look like a bird. And so another typically Simonian theme is introduced: the always very problematic *representa-tion* of reality.

The dove is a traditional symbol of love and peace, two themes notably absent from this novel. Neverthe-less, the term "dove" (Fr. *colombe*) is at the center of an important verbal cluster, since in French the word leads to some interesting puns: *Colomb* (Columbus), *colon* (settler and colon), not to mention *colonne* (column).[5] Now these words contain clues as to the country where the Palace is located, since they all refer to important episodes in the history of Spain: Christopher *Columbus*'s famous expedition across the Atlantic, financed by Queen Isabella of Spain, the subsequent *colon*ization of the New World by Spaniards, and the famous expression "Fifth *Column*" used by General Franco to refer to secret sympathizers with the Phalangist cause during the Spanish Civil War who were supposed to be found within Republican strongholds, such as Barcelona. In the novel, the official party line is that the kidnappings and political assassinations that plague the city are being perpetrated by Fifth Column infiltrators. However, there are also indications, or at least suspicions, that these political crimes may be the work of progovernment Loyalists who, for political reasons, are liquidating members of their own side. Such unconfirmed suspicions can be said to parallel the presence of the important verbal clues outlined above. One may have strong suspicions about the identities of the murderers, but there is no real proof, just as neither the city nor the country where most of the action of the novel takes place is ever explicitly named. Significantly, all the terms belonging to this verbal cluster hinge upon a word, "dove," used to describe the recurrent motif that contributes the most to the novel's structural unity: the omnipresent *pigeons* which, indifferent to the political *revolution* going on around them, fly in *circles* above the large square in front of a *palatial* hotel located in an unnamed Spanish-speaking city.[6]

In *The Palace* the emphasis is definitely not on the

psychological makeup of the characters; they are mere pretexts in Simon's exploration of the descriptive capacities of language. In fact, the Palace is more of a character than some of the human beings taking part in the drama. All three of the principal human characters are members of the so-called International Brigade: the student is French; the Rifleman, Italian; and the mocking cynic, American.

The student is divided between the present and the past. Although we learn nothing of what he has become in the fifteen years that have lapsed since the events narrated took place (probably in 1936), he seems to look upon his former self with a great deal of irony, "the student, the homunculus, the fledgling, the distant and microscopic double" (236, 215). Perhaps he has become tainted with the American's cynicism. It is notable that after the American's disappearance, the student begins to talk like him.

In his late 30s, the American represents the voice of disillusioned experience. He is talkative and undoubtedly wise in the ways of the world, especially the troubled political world of Spain during the civil war; he mocks the cause for which he is fighting, or rather the traitors to the cause whose existence he believes no one on the Republican side wishes to acknowledge. By questioning the existence of the infamous Fifth Column and its responsibilities for the death of the old general, Santiago, the American strongly insinuates that it is an imaginary construct invented by the so-called Loyalists and that it is in fact they who are secretly assassinating members of their own side for political gain. The American's questions, doubts, and mocking sarcasm may have cost him his life. Like the very existence of the Fifth Column about which he is so cynical, his disappearance is problematic. Did he go to the front to join the American battalion as the student is told, or was he taken off and shot? While the student obviously fears the latter eventuality, neither he nor the reader can be sure.

Spelled with a capital, the Rifle refers not to a thing but to a man of childlike placidity who is so inseparable from his weapon that he has become metonymically identified with it. Like his countryman Columbus, the Rifle is working for Spain, albeit in a different way. However, the Rifle's role in *The Palace* is chiefly that of a storyteller. Using a pencil and a cheap notebook, he draws diagrams to aid him in giving the student a detailed account of a political assassination that he was involved in years before the student comes to the city. The student wonders just what it is that drives someone to tell his story, whether it is to make the past more real or whether it's "to tear, to fling from himself that violence, that thing which has seized on, made use of him" (85–86, 77). In either case, both interpretations are equally valid for the novel itself. The close relationship between the narrative as a whole and the story within the story in chapter 2 is demonstrated by the fact that the Rifle's tale is embedded in the narration of the ex-student's train journey to and his arrival in the wartorn city. In what must surely be considered a great performance of narrative writing, Simon has entwined the two stories so inextricably that it is often difficult to separate them. Even more problematic is the fate of the Rifle. Is the death described at the end of the last chapter his? Is it a suicide, an accidental death, a murder, or "merely" the metaphorical death of a revolution that ends up coming back full circle to the repressive state of things as they were before? As in *The Flanders Road,* there is no simple truth, no single interpretation. The text resists all attempts to reduce it to a conventional narrative, for it is fundamentally open-ended: the fates of the American, the student, and the Rifle are as uncertain as the existence of the Fifth Column. Ambiguity is part and parcel of the act of narration in Simon.[7]

At the time of the ex-student's return to the city fifteen years after the events, the Palace has been replaced by a bank, which symbolizes the triumph of capitalism and the death of the so-called revolution. The descriptions of the hotel, which are among the most vivid in Simon's entire *oeuvre,* place the emphasis on both the gigantic size of the building and its associations with death. For example, the Palace is compared to a giant shipwreck—

[...] the whole of the enormous building now resembling, in the furtive sunbeams that sparkled on the wet roofs, making the windows flash, some monumental, streaming wreck driven from its course and abandoned by the storm, and over whose ledges the water, withdrawing, had draped the habitual debris [...] (233, 212–13)

and a huge tomb—

[...] arrogant, vertical, rococo, secret, exotic, and peopled with its mysterious phantoms of slave-trading millionaires, of traveling dowagers, of rich Brazilian ladies, of divas on tour, and of evanescent, suave, perverse and pink apparitions of surprised shepherdesses, like some monumental mausoleum, the monstrous vestige of some exquisite, barbarous and corrupt civilization long since vanished, absurd, disproportionate, unusable, the guardian [. . .] of a kind of malediction [. . .]. (206–07, 187–88)

In either case, it is clear that the Palace allows Simon to exploit the descriptive possibilities inherent in an evocative theme, which is a grand hotel fallen on hard times. The shipwreck simile develops the idea of a disaster and the concomitant association with destruction and decay, which are highlighted by the *absence* of the passengers and the eery *presence* of the "habitual debris" churned up by the ocean, which litter the vast surface of a sinking ship. In the case of the Palace, the debris makes one think of the revolutionary rhetoric to which the new inhabitants of the hotel continue to pay lip service. In the second passage the former guests in the hotel are transformed into a hoard of "mysterious phantoms" that continue to haunt the building as though it were an ancient mausoleum. Their ghostly presence will serve to curse all those, such as the ex-student, who dare venture into this sanctum sanctorum of a "barbarous and corrupt civilization." It is interesting to note that the twin themes of economic injustice and social decadence, both of which the revolution was supposed to have put an end to, allow the writer to develop an image whose textual exuberance recalls the baroque interiors of the Palace. As elsewhere in Simon, description here exists not just for the sake of ornament, but for the sake of the actual narrative, since the former allows the latter to grow and proliferate in intricate detail.

Some of the themes developed in *The Palace* include

the difficulty of storytelling, the uncertainty of human perceptions and memories, the problematic representation of movement, and the omnipresence of death and decay. In addition, aside from the principal themes, the text abounds in recurrent motifs, such as pigeons, streetcars, posters, burned-out churches, and the colors gray and yellow, all of which contribute to the novel's unity and harmony.

As for the narrative structure of *The Palace,* its five parts recall the five men in the hotel room during the central episode told in chapter 3, "The Funeral of Patroclus,"[8] the five acts of a classical tragedy, the Fifth Column, and the five panels of the baroque altar-piece which figured so prominently in the French subtitle of *The Wind.* The first and last chapters, "Inventory" and "Lost and Found," as well as the second and fourth chapters, "The Rifle's Story" and "In the Night," respectively correspond to each other in this most symmetrical of structures. For example, the doubly nocturnal tale of a political assassination in chapter 2—both the action and the telling of the tale occur at night— "contaminates" the atmosphere described in chapter 4 and contributes to the student's panic when he realizes that the American too may have become a victim to political expediency. The novel is narrated in the third person, even the Rifle's story, which is filtered through three narrative consciousnesses, the Rifle's and the student's and the narrator's. This use of the third person helps create the sense of distance that the ex-student feels between him and his former self.

As in *The Grass* where the reproduction of Marie's notebooks affects the actual presentation of the text in the 1958 novel, so too *The Palace* makes use of typographical images, in the form of short messages in Spanish printed in boldface capitals which break up both the linguistic and typographical homogeneity of the text. They visibly jump out at the reader since they form such a sharp contrast with the pages of Simon's dense descriptive prose. From a realistic point of view, these mini-texts reproduce the effect that the foreign words have on the student. Many refer to the general's death—

¡EL GIGANTE DE LA LUCHA! ... ¿QUIEN ASESINO A SANTIAGO? ... ¡EL CRIMEN HA SIDO FIRMADO! ... ¿QUIEN A MUERTO EL COMMANDANTE? ... ¿QUIEN ES EL ASESINO DE SANTIAGO? (46, 39)[9]

QUIEN HA MUERTO QUIEN HA ASESINADO QUIEN HA FIRMADO EL CRIMEN (178, 162)[10]

others to commercial signs—

BANCO INDUSTRIAL DEL NORTE (244, 223)

ANALISIS ORINA—ESPUTOS—SANGRE (163, 164, 167; 148, 149, 152)[11]

and posters—

VENCEREMOS (89, 134, 197; 81, 122, 179)[12]

While the actual import of the messages varies, from the anxious questioning of the newspaper headlines announcing a political assassination about which no one can or will tell the truth, to the highly ironic poster showing a man breaking free from the chains of servitude which supposedly no longer bind him, in all cases these short messages are untranslated and they remain pieces of alien matter which neither writer nor reader can assimilate readily. As such, they recall the beer which the ex-student drinks and which he cannot digest any more than he can digest the strange happenings to which he was once witness.[13] Even in his use of typography, Simon has succeeded in describing in a manner at once graphic and vivid the troubling question at the center of the novel: the elusive "facts" about which it is possible to know so little because they always remain as alien and alienating as the nameless city where the (ex-)student finds himself twice caught up in a whirligig of perceptions, impressions, and memories.

The first-time reader of *The Palace* may not succeed in deciphering all the historical allusions, hidden clues, and verbal connotations contained in the novel. This is not absolutely necessary. To be sure, most of the narrative threads of such a textually dense novel are already present in its first pages where they are waiting to be unraveled by the attentive reader. But meaning in this novel, like Simon's other works, is largely a cumulative process to be savored slowly, especially in the re-reading of the text. None of Simon's novels could be considered an easy read, since they usually require some background knowledge of European history, and they always require an appreciation of the evocative powers of language. But once the reader makes the necessary effort to decipher *The Palace,* the reading will provide ample reward as more and more pieces of this intricate puzzle gradually begin to fit together.

NOTES

1. See George Orwell, *Homage to Catalonia* (New York: Harcourt, 1952), pp. 150–79.

2. Simon himself has said, "No, it isn't a book about the Spanish Revolution. It's a book about 'my' revolution. The Spanish Revolution? To speak about it properly, one would have to go through archives for years. You would have do the work of an historian. A novelist can only have a subjective, partial and, consequently, false view of things" ("Entretien: Claude Simon parle," *L'Express,* [Apr. 5, 1962], quoted by Sykes in *Les Romans de Claude Simon,* p. 87 [My trans.]).

3. While not actually described in *The Palace,* desk and dictionary will appear at the end of Simon's later novel, *The Battle of Pharsalus.* Also, *Orion aveugle* includes a drawing by Simon of just such a scene.

4. *The Palace,* trans. Richard Howard (New York: Braziller, 1963), p. 13; *Le Palace* (Paris: Minuit, 1962), p. 9. Subsequent references will appear in parentheses.

5. Cf. Jean-Pierre Vidal's article, "*Le Palace,* palais des mirages intestins ou l'auberge espagnole," *Etudes littéraires* 9.1 (1976): 189–214. Vidal points out the generative function of the name of the hotel described in Simon's 1947 text, *Colon,* which is the probable model of the hotel in *The Palace.* Although the name of the hotel is not mentioned in the 1962 novel, the name of a streetcar stop called "Colon" is (136, 123). As for the anatomical echo, a civil war is also known as a *guerre intestine* in French.

6. Cf."(the column itself constituting the axis of the indefatigable and oscillating revolution, of the permanent whirlwind of wings suspended in the sultry air, describing an invisible inverted cone, the point at the bottom): a dove, the bird, the spirit perched there in a shudder of fire and feathers like a sign" (95, 86).

7. In *The French New Novel* (London: Oxford UP, 1969), John Sturrock contends that the death at the end of the narrative is the student's suicide (pp. 53, 62), although in his later edition of the novel (London: Methuen, 1972), he changes his mind (p. xxiv), and is thus in agreement with Vivian Mercier who contends that it is the Rifle's death (*The New Novel From Queneau to Pinget* [New York: Farrar, Straus, 1971], p. 304). Jiménez-Fajardo writes, "[A]ll indications point merely to a metaphorical death. There is no structural neces-

sity for a true suicide" (*Claude Simon* [Boston: Twayne, 1975], p. 196n). Cf. Doris Kadish, "From the Narration of Crime to the Crime of Narration: Claude Simon's *Le Palace*," *The International Fiction Review,* 4 (1977): 128–36.

8. Chapter 3 narrates the perceptions of the student—three days after his arrival in the city—as he looks down from a window in the Palace at the funeral of the assassinated Republican general. As for the original Patroclus, he was a hero in the Trojan War. The friend and right-hand man of Achilles, he was killed by Hector; Achilles held a great funeral for his friend after he got the body back from the Trojans (*Iliad,* Book 23). Given the probable circumstances of Santiago's death, the title is ironic. In terms of models, the funeral procession appears to have been inspired by that held for Buenaventura y Domingo Durruti (1896–1936), a photo of which can be found in the volume of *Entretiens* devoted to Simon.

9. "The giant of the struggle! Who assassinated Santiago? The crime has been signed! Who killed the Commander? Who is Santiago's assassin?" The mistakes in Spanish may be due to the student's imperfect mastery of the language.

10. "Who has killed who has assassinated who has signed the crime"

11. "Analysis: Urine—Sputum—Blood"

12. "We shall overcome"

13. The beer motif is doubly evocative in the original text since the French word *bière* also means "coffin." Significantly, the novel ends with the image of the boxes of shoeshine boys who work in an underground washroom near the site of the old Palace. The boxes resemble "antique and mysterious coffers, tiny and absurd children's coffins" (252, 230).

85

CHAPTER FIVE

Histoire

In 1967, at age 54, Claude Simon received the famous Prix Médicis for his novel, *Histoire,* a long and intriguing work that tells the story of a day in the life of a middle-aged man who sees himself as a "harmless idiot." Although the events of the day in question are quite ordinary, the novel ranges far and wide in terms of historical and geographical detail. Moreover, the novel is chockfull of literary allusions to modern and classical texts. *Histoire* will be easier to follow for readers already familiar with the author's three previous novels; for all readers undoubtedly it will carry the strongest emotional impact of any of Simon's novels published in the 1960s and 1970s.

Whereas *The Grass* and *The Flanders Road* tell the story of the Thomases, *Histoire* tells an equally intriguing but more far-reaching tale of the family, life, and times of the ex-student in *The Palace* who, it turns out, is the first cousin of Corinne in *The Flanders Road*. Georges Thomas was Corinne's cousin by marriage, and the narrator of *Histoire* grew up in the same house as his younger cousin; like Georges he appears to have been very attracted to the sensual young woman who married a man twenty years her senior, Captain de Reixach. It may help to think of the fictional landscape of the Reixach Cycle as a giant canvas, only parts of which had already been covered by

86

the earlier novels. *Histoire,* whose deliberately ambiguous French title was retained by Richard Howard
for his English translation of the novel, explores some
of these potentially rich areas of the fictional canvas,
which remained to be filled in. One must bear in mind
that while the five novels published between 1958 and
1969 constitute a kind of novelistic quintet, the stories
of these reappearing characters do not form a totally
coherent whole. Like any organic being, whether plant
or animal, the cycle has just grown, so to speak, as one
novel led to another. Simon himself has said that his
novels come out of each other.[1] Rather than concen-
trate on any possible inconsistencies as weaknesses or
faults which the author ought to have "corrected,"
readers of Simon's Reixach Cycle should appreciate
such zones of narrative tension for what they really
are: vivid proof of the ongoing dynamics involved in
writing novels of such length, breadth, and complexity.

Told in the first person by an anonymous narrator,
Histoire presents the reader with a challenge, for it is
encyclopedic in its scope and range of subject matter.
One might liken it to a huge collage or a patchwork
quilt composed of many heterogeneous parts, including
a cast of some forty characters if one includes the ex-
tras. Like Joyce's *Ulysses,* upon which it is modeled to
a certain extent, the narrative in *Histoire* is structured
around the activities of the protagonist—a modern Everyman who returns to the old family home in southern France in the early 1960s—during one day in his
very unheroic life. At one level, apparently little of
great import happens, while at another elements of the
narrator's entire past as well as that of his family and
country are worked into the novel. At the same time,

Histoire is a mystery that never quite divulges the answer to the central enigma it poses concerning the fate of the narrator's wife, Hélène.

The word *histoire* paradoxically refers to both nonfiction *and* fiction, a curious combination since normally history passes itself off as the truth and fiction is considered to be pure invention, the stuff of storytellers' imaginations. Here the two combine and overlap in what is an inherently polysemic word in French. Furthermore, it is interesting to note that, as in English, *histoire* refers, not only to the actual events of the past, but also to a book that recounts such events. Written with a capital, *Histoire* could well be the title of a textbook of ancient, modern, or sacred history: a book in which the haphazard and chaotic events of the past are ordered in a supposedly coherent narrative based on the twin props of chronology and rhetoric. Simon's *Histoire* is an antihistory par excellence since the ordering of narrative sequences is only partially governed by temporal criteria and since it refuses to have recourse to the comfortable rhetoric of expository prose, a rhetoric which is not all that different from conventional novels. The word *histoire* is also synonymous with "lie," as in the expression "tall tale"—in French "tu me racontes des histoires" [lit. "you are telling me stories"] means "you're pulling my leg." As well, the word means "thingamajig" or "whatsit," something which cannot be named.[2] Finally, as Simon himself has pointed out, the word's Greek cognate, *istoria,* means "search" or "quest."[3] Thus the title of this novel promises the reader a *search* that could well turn out to be more important than the actual results or product of such an effort, here the quest for knowledge about the past. Paradoxically, by Simon's use of the name of an academic subject and discipline grounded in archival research, he warns us that the novel we are about to read is "just" a story, a kind of *lie,* and that it may well contain *lacunae,* those *thingamajigs* that cannot or will not be named by the *narrative* upon which the reader is about to embark.

"It submerges us. We organize it. It falls to pieces. We organize it again and fall to pieces ourselves." Simon chose to begin *Histoire* with this quotation from the *Duino Elegies* (1912–22) by the Austrian poet Rainer Maria Rilke (1875–1926).[4] It recalls the epigraph of *The Wind,*[5] except that in this case the disorder, the falling to pieces, affects *us.* In Simonian terms that which submerges us is the past, our own individual pasts and the collective past of mankind. Both apply to the protagonist of *Histoire* and to his efforts as narrator to bring some order to the many memories which invade his consciousness while he goes about his daily life. No doubt such is the actual experience of Simon's readers: while reading *Histoire,* they will remember their own past—the archetypal family photo album each of us carries in our memory—and at the same time they will have to come to terms with the novel as a novel, to bring a certain order to this very mixed bag of memories and emotions, of words and images. How then is one to think or speak of such a multifarious novel in anything even resembling an orderly or organized manner? There is always the risk that one will be submerged by it, that any effort to organize the raw material of the narrative will be to no avail, or worse.

Located in an unnamed provincial town in southern

France, the house referred to at the outset of the novel is the one where the narrator grew up and to which he has returned many years later. The house is a fitting metaphor for the collection of memories the narrator associates with it and its former inhabitants (most of whom are dead at the time of the narrative present):

> One of them was almost touching the house and in summer when I worked late into the night sitting in front of the open window I could see it or at least its farthest twigs in the lamplight with their feathery leaves trembling faintly against the darkness beyond, the oval folioles dyed a raw unreal green by the electric light stirring occasionally like plumes as though suddenly animated by a movement of their own (and behind you could discern transmitted by degrees a mysterious and delicate murmur spreading invisibly through the dim tangle of branches) [. . .].[6]

In the opening sequence, "one of them" is totally ambiguous at the first reading of the text. One might be tempted to think that the sentence is about a leaf because leaves are mentioned later on. However, this is not the intent of the passage since the only logical reference for "them" is *branches,* which does not occur until several lines farther on into the text. Already from this initial segment, it is clear that the narrative will be told in the first person, which posits a narrative duality, for there is not only the "I" of what is being narrated—working at night, the tree branch, and the like—but also the "I" who is performing the narration, at some later point in time.

Just as the text will soon reprise the image of a tree

in the form of a family tree, in this case that of the former royal family of France as it was graphically illustrated in one of the narrator's old history books, so too the narrative will return to the now familiar Simonian leitmotif of birds, implicitly present in the opening sequence. Feathers, plumes, "a mysterious and delicate murmur"—all prepare the reader for the invisible presence of a multitude of birds, which, like spirits shrouded in the branches of the "family tree," are always already there waiting to be discovered. The faint murmur of the birds will lead inevitably to the mnemonic presence of old ladies, the "old birds," who used to visit the narrator's grandmother when he was a child.[7] However, that is not all. The tiny leaves of the tree are compared to feathers, which are used in making plumed hats as well as in writing (*plume* means both "feather" and "pen" in French), that is, for the inscription of letters and words on sheets or *leaves* of paper. Thus it is clear that if the sentence is ostensibly about the branch of the tree that touched the window of the room in which the narrator used to engage in some kind of mysterious work late at night, the sentence is also *implicitly* about the task the narrator is currently performing, the writing of the very text that we are reading.

Just as the small leaves are part of a larger whole— the branches, the trunk, and, of course, the entire tree—so too words lead to other words, and small bits and pieces of text, such as this fragment, lead to larger chunks of text, whole narrative sequences or chapters and, in the end, the entire narrative itself, the novel. What is more, just as the delicate and invisible murmur in the dark is communicated from leaf to leaf,

91

from branch to branch, so too the meaning of the text is communicated to the readers delicately, gradually. Thus we are brought back to the title, *Histoire* as story *and* as text, the dual character of all narrative. We begin to suspect that this is a story told at two levels, that of the *fiction* as well as that of its *telling*. It is a proof of Simon's great talent as a writer that these two tales of fictional and textual arborescence are so entirely fused into one another that the reader deciphers both of them simultaneously, almost effortlessly.[8]

To understand the relationships linking the main characters in *Histoire* and Simon's next novel, *The Battle of Pharsalus,* a family tree may be of some help. It should be remembered that at the time of the narrative present in *Histoire* most of the characters only exist as memories in the narrator's mind. The narrator's father died in World War I; de Reixach in World War II; the mother, Charles's wife and the grandmother between the wars; Charles probably died after the Second World War. Although it is difficult to piece together Hélène's story, she and the narrator last saw each other some time before the action of the novel begins in about 1960.

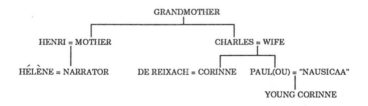

The grandmother remains a secondary character chiefly remembered for the eternal tears she shed over the many disasters that plagued the family, including her own daughter's death. Indeed, one of the most vivid scenes in *Histoire* describes the last rites of the narrator's mother when he recalls seeing his grandmother kneeling beside him to receive communion:

> [. . .] close to me the old faded pitiful face stretched forward, eyes closed, the half-open mouth obscenely releasing that thick tongue with its rough papillae which, though she kept her eyelids closed, still stuck out to receive like a gumdrop the white wafer which she nimbly ingested with an intense expression of suffering and greedy beatitude [. . .]. (5, 14)

As is typical in Simon, the scene is *visualized* more than it is narrated, for the actual content is the byproduct of the description. Often Simon concentrates on just one part of a character's body—here the grandmother is reduced to her face—as though that one physical feature were the quintessential attribute of that person's life and personality. The grandmother's past and present sufferings, both real and imagined, her naïve religious faith, the sensual gratification that she receives by taking the consecrated bread, the body of Christ, in her mouth, as well as her need to demonstrate outwardly the feelings of beatitude she was taught in her own childhood to be appropriate on such occasions—all of this goes into the makeup of the grandmother as a character. However, what would lead in many novelists to a psychological portrait of Grand-mère must here be deduced from a concrete description in which the narrator adopts the point of view of his younger self. In other words, like the other characters in *Histoire,* the grandmother has become the description of a memory in which visual elements predominate.

The narrator has no personal memories of his father who presumably died shortly before or after his son's birth. Thus the narrator knows his father only from the enlarged photograph that hung in his mother's bedroom where Henri "presided" over her sickness and death like some forever youthful god: "that sepia enlargement which she stared at from her deathbed, with its silky sepia beard, its tufted eyebrows, that bold, joyous, eternally young expression, both mocking and indulgent" (213, 253). During the years of their long engagement at the beginning of the century, Henri sent his fiancée numerous postcards from all over the Orient. His cold, laconic messages sometimes included information of a didactic nature as though he thought it his manly duty to teach his future wife the names of the interesting places he visited and lived in. The postcards are now part of a huge pile which the narrator discovers while cleaning out an old chest of drawers in the family home to which he has returned. Initially they allow him to escape the confines of his own personal situation by imagining and fantasizing about the exotic places shown in the photos. Since these were taken at a time when the socio-economic and political hierarchy established by and for European white males was supposed to last forever, the postcards illustrate a calm, orderly universe. At first, the detailed descriptions of ocean steamers and exotic outposts of empire may seem redolent with nostalgia for a time when the world was a simpler and better-organized place. But some of the narrator's comments clearly indicate his suspicions that the postcards are barely disguised evidence of the white man's economic and sexual exploitation of the indigenous populations of British and French colonial possessions. Certainly, Henri's world had all the appearances of a simple one: his future wife stayed at home where her only task was to be beautiful and to await his return while he crisscrossed the globe in the service of his country. In fact, of course, their orderly universe was based upon a kind of grand illusion about everything and everybody being all right, since it already contained the seeds of its own destruction: the outbreak of a worldwide conflict involving rival empires in which Henri was to be killed, and the subsequent onset of the mother's fatal illness. The father figure is thus always an absent presence, for he is either abroad or dead, which comes to the same thing in the mother's mind since she tends to imagine paradise as some sort of oriental colony filled with luxuriant vegetation. As for the narrator's search for his identity, his past, it is in part a search for his dead father. However, it is a search that leads nowhere, except to another postcard, sent by one of Henri's fellow officers, showing a military graveyard. In the final analysis, Henri is unknown and unknowable, an imaginary construct, which has repercussions on the way the narrator sees himself. As the critic A. C. Pugh writes, "[T]o be the child of an imaginary father is to be, in a sense, an imaginary child, and to be a prey to fantasies of de-realisation."[9]

The narrator's mother is closely associated with the Spanish motif and the theme of death in *Histoire,* for one of her principal passions was all things Spanish including bullfights, which she used to enjoy in the company of her penpal, Ninita, on visits to Barcelona. The narrator imagines his mother as intrinsically passive; time for her was endlessly repetitive, virtually static, and her chief pleasures were vicarious, since she only lived through and for her fiancé's travels and adventures.

> [...] contemplating with that calm velvety vacant vaguely dreamy gaze the pyramids, the Victorian equatorial cities and impenetrable forests, resembling [...] one of those heroines of theater or actually of opera a druidess or paladin's bride, a little plump like those imposing and virginal sopranos [...]. (19, 30)

The last sequence of the novel dates back to the two-year period of conjugal bliss when his parents traveled together in the Orient. The narrator figures out that it was during this extended honeymoon that he was conceived, hence the image of his pregnant mother writing a postcard to her own mother from an island appropriately called Félicité.[10] As for the narrator's personal memories of his mother, he only remembers her when she was sick and dying, probably from tuberculosis. Her illness did not prevent her from keeping up with the pretence of normalcy and social ritual in the form of the musical evenings she insisted on holding even after she was too weak to walk. A staunch Catholic, the mother has a baroque and superstitious faith in the godhead, whether it be the divinity or her late husband. On the other hand, the mother is not remembered lovingly by the narrator. Rather, her son appears to have been frightened and repulsed by the grotesque figure she cut while dying, for in her son's eyes she had already become a cold, inanimate object. Again and again throughout the novel, the mother's ravaged body is associated with a knife, "[. . .] silhouetted against the white of the festooned pillows her face like a knifeblade seen from the side the nose too like a knifeblade and above it on each side the shining black eyes [. . .]" (8, 16–17). From the tone and tenor of the narrative in *Histoire,* it is clear that for the narrator his mother had no maternal qualities. He imagines her in her youth as an empty-headed social butterfly and remembers her in her maturity as an impersonal, reified, and dangerous-looking entity. At least this is what he has internalized, what remains of her in him. Long after her death at age forty-five, the narrator's memory of his mother exerts a strong hold on his imagination, for he seems to be both afraid of and fascinated by this incarnation of the castrating female. From beyond the grave the mother still has the powerful capacity to *cut* her son off from any future possible happiness with another woman, such as Hélène, in order to assimilate him to the "sacred" family traditions of solitude and widowhood.[11]

Uncle Charles plays the role of both surrogate parent and alter ego to the narrator. As a young adult, Charles lives a bohemian existence in Paris where he concerns himself with such mysterious activities as poetry and art. Years later, after the death of his wife, Charles returns to the family property in the south of France. There he occupies himself for many years with the running of the vineyard and with helping raise the narrator as well as his own two children, Corinne and Paulou, neither of whom he seems to have anything in common with. To a certain extent, Charles unites and (re)incarnates the activities and the values associated in *The Grass* and *The Flanders Road* with Georges Thomas's grandfather and father respectively, that is, farming and writing.[12] At the same time, Charles also resembles Georges in his views concerning the value of traditional book learning, or rather the lack of it. Charles expresses a cynical opinion about the capacity of language and art to deal adequately with the past, to capture or represent with any kind of accuracy the motley and disturbing nature of the experiences one has lived through.

> ... between reading it in books or seeing it artistically represented in museums and touching it and being splashed by it comes to the same difference that exists between seeing the word *shell* written and finding yourself from one moment to the next hugging the ground and the ground itself where the sky should be and the air itself splattering around you [. . .] at that moment the word *shell* or the word *explosion* exists no more than the word *ground* or *sky* or *fire,* which means you can no more tell such things than you can experience them again afterwards [. . .]. (125–26, 152)

At the same time, even after this indictment, Charles concludes "and yet you have only words, so all you can try to do . . . ."[13] In a word, Charles is a living contradiction wrapped up in an enigma: Did he really have an affair with the model of an artist named Van Velden? Did this affair lead to his wife's suicide from an overdose of barbiturates? And is this the reason why he spends all his days shut up in an untidy office with the shutters closed as though he must deny all light, all life? The answers to these and other questions are not provided by the text of *Histoire*. Like the narrator, all the reader can do is speculate about this kind of novel within a novel; furthermore, it is a novel that refuses the telling just as one of the meanings of the title promised, since *Histoire* is (also) the unnamed and unnameable "truth" that eludes our grasp, as Charles demonstrates in the passage quoted. What is clear is that Charles is the narrator's double, for the latter's story presents a disturbing parallel with his uncle's.

The narrator himself remains a highly problematic character because he narrates his own story. Within the context of the Reixach Cycle, it is possible to identify him with the ex-student in *The Palace*. And like Georges in *The Flanders Road,* the narrator in *Histoire* was in the cavalry. Furthermore, he describes one scene in a POW camp that could have been taken from the earlier novel (47, 61). And as Montès was characterized in *The Wind* the narrator refers to himself, at least as he thinks others see him, as an idiot. Suffice it to say that the narrator in *Histoire,* whom we will meet again in *The Battle of Pharsalus* and *The Georgics,* is a combination of many traits and stories that Simon had already used or would use again in other novels. The first-person narrator of the 1967 novel is both a character, the sum of past and present experiences not all of which will ever become clear in the reader's mind, *and* a writer who puts words together in an evocative manner so that meaning is produced by verbal associations, linear juxtapositions, and sequential transitions. As becomes progressively clearer while one reads the novel, the latter function often takes precedence over the former since, in *Histoire,* it is the *poetic* function of language that predominates. As such, any study of the narrator in this novel leads inevitably to a study of the narrative itself, whether in thematic, stylistic, or narratological terms.

Nevertheless, one can discern certain traits which, when put together, could be said to constitute the character of the narrator. First and foremost, he is a creature of the past, of his own and others' pasts. Despite his concerns about money, there is no mention of the future and the present is remarkable only for its banality as he goes about his activites during the day which forms the backdrop to his "remembrance of things past." In terms of social, political, financial, and personal endeavors, the narrator could be compared unfavorably to his more successful peers Paul, Corinne, and Lambert, not to mention the heroes whom he read about in his adolescence.[14] The narrator's not so revolutionary activities in Spain during the civil war and the end of his marriage to Hélène leave one with the impression that he sees himself as a failure at all levels.[15] He is particularly tormented by what seem to be remorseful memories of his failed marriage. Interestingly, the narrator compares himself to Hercules who was killed by a poisoned shirt sent to him by his wife, Dejaneira. "I wish I wish I wish if I could just take it off tear it off to regain coolness oblivion Dejaneira" (309, 365, trans. alt.). The metaphorical shirt represents painful memories he cannot seem to forget. In fact, one could consider the entire novel an attempt by the narrator to sublimate his pain by writing down his and Hélène's story even though it refuses any simple or straightforward telling.[16]

Any "portrait" of the narrator is further complicated by the numerous similarities that exist between him and his uncle. Charles seems to know the narrator and his story so well that he is able to tell the younger man what he (the narrator) experienced in Spain during the war.[17] And in chapters 9 and 10 the narrator literally puts himself in his uncle's shoes after finding a photo of Charles having tea in an artist's studio with several other people, including a naked female model. The narrator scrutinizes this memento of Charles's bohemian life so intensely that he ends by imagining what preceded and followed the taking of the photo. Ultimately, the perspective changes as the narrator identifies so closely with his uncle that he adopts the pronoun "I" while referring to the person previously identifed as Charles. Now the "I" is sexually attracted to the model in the photo, and the breakdown of his marriage is attributed to an extramarital affair that "I" had with a young woman, probably the model. This blurring of the identities of Charles and his nephew has further repercussions since it entails a concomitant blurring of Hélène and Charles's unnamed wife in the last chapter of the novel when the narrator remembers and/or imagines the pathetic scene of an estranged couple lying side by side on the deathbed of their marriage so to speak. It is impossible to tell if the narrator is merely putting himself in the skin of his uncle and/or if their stories are indeed similar or even identical. The ambiguity is anchored in the narrative, and no amount of close textual analysis of *Histoire* will allow the reader to adopt one or another reading as the definitive meaning of the novel.

What is especially interesting is that rather than

diminishing the significance of the text this ambiguity contributes to it. Characters in *Histoire* remain walled up in their emotions, whether it be the narrator's father who limits himself to the most laconic of messages on the postcards sent to his fiancée or Charles who shuts himself off from the world in his darkened office. The blurring and eventual merging of the stories of uncle and nephew allow the narrator at one and the same time to articulate and conceal a crucial part of his story. Furthermore, the emotional content of *Histoire* is heightened, not lessened, by such a deliberate subversion of traditional novel writing techniques, as evidenced by the following passage:

> *veuf* [widower] a crippled truncated word remaining somehow in suspense cut off against nature like the English *half* divided *cut off* from something missing suddenly in the mouth the lips pronouncing VF still making the fff like a sound of rustling air torn by the swift glistening and murderous passage of a blade. (65, 82, trans. alt.)[18]

Here the very word *veuf* becomes a horrible onomatopoeia of the knife blow that cuts the widower off from all future happiness, leaving him a physical and emotional cripple. It is as though he has been wounded (castrated) by the very same blow that may have been self-inflicted by the beloved upon her body in a desperate attempt to escape a doomed marriage. While the passage seems to refer to Charles, it can also be read as a telling self-portrait by the narrator, for the sense of loss, the acute pain and suffering have been internalized, not just in psychological but also textual terms.

Hélène, the most important person in the narrator's emotional life, is associated with Greece, sexual pleasure, and the inherently unattainable nature of a significant other whom one can never really know. The beginnings of the breakdown of their marriage seem to occur even during their honeymoon. "[. . .] all I could see was her blond hair her back like an enigmatic wall enclosing hiding that kind of tragic melancholy that black somber thing that was already inside her like a core of death concealed like a poison a poignard [. . .]" (89, 109–10). Like many of the male characters, Hélène is destined to remain a puzzling enigma. However, unlike Charles, the narrator never attempts to adopt her point of view since she remains an object, albeit a beautiful one, a pure vision of sensual and chromatic delight. She is associated with the sea, the fruits of the earth, and the tears which welled up in her eyes when the narrator last saw her as she prepared to leave for Barcelona by train: "and nothing but her eyes what do you call that phenomenon that keeps liquids from lakes of tears" (29, 40). Given Hélène's early love of and affinity for Greece, it seems entirely fitting that the end of their marriage should see her drawn into the sphere of Spain, which is itself linked with the theme of death. At the same time, the "lakes of tears" form an implicit link with all the other lakes that are mentioned in the novel, including Lake Stymphalus in Greece and its monstrous birds which the narrator dreams in the second chapter are tearing his flesh apart, just as the memory of Hélène comes back to haunt him during his day's activities.[19] Another recurring motif which seems to be related to Hélène is a newspaper headline describing a woman who committed suicide by jumping out of a fourth-story window. Although it is nowhere stated in *Histoire* that Hélène did indeed kill herself, the many clues that are scattered throughout the novel indicate this may have been the case.[20] As the narrative progresses, more and more half-veiled allusions, thematic associations, and verbal echoes can be linked to Hélène, so that "[a]t the end of the novel, the text will be so suffused with connotations leading directly to Hélène that [the narrator] will no longer be able to avoid the most painful episodes he had tried to suppress."[21] Hence the narrator's longing for a calm, peaceful Alpine lake surrounded by snow-covered mountains to which he would like to escape as though to cleanse and cool his troubled soul. Or the envy-triggered associations about Greece when he visits Paul and his beautiful wife, a modern Nausicaa, at their seaside summer home on the Mediterranean (ch. [11]). There one of the guests is a Greek businessman, which makes the narrator recall that an ancient Greek ship lies at the bottom of the sea nearby. Furthermore, the sight of a dead squid leads to the twice repeated vision of the dead body of Hector being dragged behind Achilles's chariot, as told in the *Iliad,* that ancient tale of a war fought over *Helen* of Troy. Paradoxically, it is as though Hélène were destined to be present everywhere in a narrative that refuses to tell her story forthright, not only her fate but also her point of view. Readers will recall the problematic destiny of the Rifle in *The Palace* as well as the suspected but unprovable suicide of de Reixach in *The Flanders Road.* In a similar way, *Histoire* is a mystery novel that provides no facile solution. But unlike the two earlier works, in this novel the lacuna around which the suspense is created is largely responsible for the *emotional impact* that the narrative has on the reader. In the final analysis, *Histoire* is the tale of a love not so much lost as inscribed and written, however painfully, in the proverbial heart of the matter, the verbal tissue of the narrative.

Histoire is structured at several different levels. The first level consists of the 12 unnumbered and untitled sections or chapters which correspond to 24 hours in the life of the narrator.[22] After an introductory chapter, similar in function to that of an overture to an opera in which the principal themes and techniques are introduced, the subsequent chapters follow in chronological order the events of the narrator's day: three chapters cover the morning's activities, two are devoted to lunch, four to the afternoon, and the last two chapters cover the evening and night hours. Although such a structure may seem natural, it is in fact inlaid with numerous literary parallels and allusions. A day in the life of a modern antihero recalls Joyce's *Ulysses,* as well as the *Odyssey* and the *Iliad* of Homer, both of which are divided into 24 parts. The 12 parts of *Histoire* recall of course the 12 months of the year, the 12 signs of the zodiac, the 12 apostles—not to mention the 12 persons already present at the summer home of the narrator's cousin when he arrives there. More importantly, Lucius in Apuleius's *The Golden Ass* remained in his donkey's skin 12 months; John Reed's *Ten Days* ... contains 12 chapters; and, above all, Hercules had to perform 12 labors to expiate a murder. All these allusions have a special significance within the context of *Histoire,* so that the dual structure (24 hours; 12 parts) already allows the reader to organize the subject matter of a novel which at first glance (and quite falsely) may seem to be totally chaotic.

Another structural level is provided by the reappearance of characters, not only throughout the various sections of the novel but also from other novels by Simon, such as Corinne from *The Flanders Road*. Given Simon's penchant for using ambiguous pronouns, the initial attribution of dialogue and descriptive sequences to this or that character is an important part of the reading process. The thematic structure of *Histoire* also allows readers to make sense of the narrative and to group together the various textual manifestations of such typically Simonian themes as love, war, history, death, and memory. And other themes taken from daily life, such as food, money, and sex, provide significant clues when reading the novel. Finally, the recurrence throughout the entire text of quotations, symmetrical structures—the novel can be read as a kind of textual mixed doubles—and of typographical images, such as newspaper headlines and signs, helps readers find their ways through the vast amount of material that they have to deal with if they are to understand and enjoy the novel.

Some of the most significant patterns in *Histoire* are provided by the chromatic leitmotifs which make the descriptions so vivid. In Simon colors serve to textually bind together any number of different characters and disparate scenes. For example, yellow is the color of the wallpaper in the *salon* of the old family home where the mother insisted on entertaining despite the advanced stage of her illness. However, yellow is also the color of the earth at the grave of Charles's wife, of

106

Barcelona—not only the buildings in the city but also the dirty tramp steamers in the harbor—of the old photos taken by the mother in Spain, of the tips of the smoke stacks of the small steamers that ply the waters of the unnamed lake to which the narrator would like to escape, and of the skin of the shop owner on Félicité Island where the mother-to-be of the narrator writes a postcard to her own mother. Black is attached to the rapacious antique dealer who covets the narrator's old furniture at a time when he is singularly alone, but also of the dead fish that becomes a children's plaything, and which itself suggests the image of a torn and mutilated body. On the other hand, white is associated with life and life-giving experiences, in particular an Alpine lake, northern climes, and the healthy, full-breasted women who inhabit them, moonlight, milky skin, and an early sexual adventure. Brown is associated with the eyes of the young model who used to pose for the painter, but also with the two Corinnes, Paul's sister and his daughter, the former's namesake. Traces of teeth marks in a chocolate bar and chocolate-stained lips carry strong erotic connotations, all of which seem to come back to the naked model in the photo of the artist's studio. Hélène conjures up images of brightly colored dresses and, more importantly, peaches, as the narrator recalls in maddening detail all the various hues of his beloved's beautiful body, including white, yellow, and red.

In fact, the color which occurs the most frequently and which has the greatest significance is red and its various shades. The drops of red blood embroidered on the chasuble of the priest who officiates at the last rites of the narrator's mother are but an early indication of a chromatic motif that recurs again and again throughout *Histoire*. Red is associated with the cherries that Corinne and the young narrator pick in the garden of the family home. The color is linked here with an awakening sexuality on the narrator's part as well as the strong desire he feels for his cousin. Hence, the detailed description of the trace of blood on Corinne's scratched leg which anticipates another outdoors scene when several years later the narrator deflowers a willing virgin during his military service. At the same time, both the name and color of the fruit picked in that prelapsarian world of the family house and garden are linked to the bright red lipstick of one of the more original of the grandmother's friends, a member of the Reixach clan, Baronne *Cerise* (lit. "Baroness Cherry"). Later when Corinne makes her husband race horses, the famous colors of the old aristocrat, which included a cerise cap, are replaced by outrageous pink silks and a black cap. Red cherries and red lips are found on a commercial calendar in Uncle Charles's office. Moreover, red is also in the intertextual quotations from Reed's book about the Russian Revolution where he speaks with heroic rhetoric of the role played by Red Guards. This recalls the small wound the narrator receives while observing an episode of internecine squabbling in Barcelona at the time of the civil war. At the time of the narrative present, the red ink of the menu in the restaurant where the narrator eats lunch and the red berets of the soldiers in a cafe where he has a sandwich in the evening underscore the virtual omnipresence of the color in the novel. For example, the letters of the caption on the mother's postcard sent from Félicité Island can only be red. Red is the color that links much of the narrative together, for it is associated with not only sensual delight but also pain and suffering. Does the narrator feel he has blood on his hands? Like Lady Macbeth, he cannot seem to wash away the guilt and remorse he feels about his responsibility (whatever it was) in the breakdown of his marriage with Hélène. As always in Simon, structure is part and parcel of meaning, especially when the meaning resists any straightforward telling.

Histoire is a novel in which the banal and the ordinary have been infused with meaning, for everything is connected to everything else. Hence, even in the pages of apparently neutral prose describing the narrator's activities during the 24-hour period which the narrative covers, themes, images, colors, and words take on a life of their own. Not only does Simon's highly descriptive style of writing allow readers to visualize the scenes narrated but more importantly each fragment, each segment—each branch of text— leads to another to which it is joined in the majestic arborescence that makes up this narrative.

NOTES

1. "My books come out of each other like nesting tables. I wouldn't have been able to write *Histoire* without having written *The Palace,* or *The Palace* without *The Flanders Road.* In general, it's with what couldn't be said in the earlier books that I begin a new novel" (Interview with Thérèse de Saint-Phalle, "Claude Simon, franc-tireur de la révolution romanesque," *Le Figaro littéraire* [Apr. 6, 1967], p. 6 my trans.).

2. See Simon interview in *La Quinzaine littéraire* (Dec. 15–31, 1967): 4.

3. Bettina Knapp, "Interview with Claude Simon," *Kentucky Romance Review,* 16.2 (1969): 189.

4. *Uns überfüllts. Wir ordnens. Es zerfällt.*

Wir ordnens wieder und zerfallen selbst.

From "The Eighth Elegy" in *Duino Elegies* by R. M. Rilke, lines 68–69. Some of the significant themes in this elegy are leave-taking, death, and memory, all of which appear in Simon's novel. Moreover, the same elegy compares birds to "womb-born thing[s]." Considering that birds and the foetus in the mother's womb are described respectively at the beginning and end of *Histoire,* one may say that the text from which the novel's epigraph is taken has a truly "generative" function.

5. "The world is incessantly threatened by two dangers: order and disorder."

6. *Histoire,* trans. Richard Howard (New York: Braziller, 1968), p. 1; *Histoire* (Paris: Minuit, 1967), p. 9. Subsequent references will appear in parentheses in the text.

7. Later the narrator will associate the old ladies with the monstrous birds of Lake Stymphalus which Hercules had to kill as his fifth task.

8. "It is the process of transition (ramifications of textual elements) that is emblematically represented by the tree (the tree in front of the house and the genealogical tree) of which both the branches and the network of family relationships are described" (Gérard Roubichou, "*Histoire* or the Serial Novel" in *Orion Blinded,* ed. Randi Birn and Karen Gould [Lewisburg: Bucknell UP, 1981], p. 176).

9. Anthony Pugh, *Simon: "Histoire"* (London: Grant, 1982), p. 55.

10. Cf. "that bosom which already perhaps was bearing me in its shadowy tabernacle a kind of gelatinous tadpole coiled around itself with its two enormous eyes its silkworm head its toothless mouth its cartilaginous insect's forehead, me? . . . " (341, 402).

11. Cf. Pugh, *Simon: "Histoire,"* pp. 53–54; Ralph Sarkonak, *Claude Simon: les carrefours du texte* (Toronto: Editions Paratexte, 1986), pp. 139–42.

12. See Gérard Roubichou, *Lecture de "L'Herbe" de Claude Simon* (Lausanne: L'Age d'Homme, 1976), p. 286n.

13. Charles functions here as a kind of spokesman for Simon himself regarding the *mimetic* quality of literature (cf. Sarkonak, *Claude*

Simon: les carrefours du texte, pp. 35–38). What Charles does not underline (and Simon's own writing does) is the *associative* properties of langugage, the capacity that words have for calling to mind and to the page other words in a kind of verbal logic that is more akin to the art of *collage* than to photography.

14. The erotic passages quoted in Latin in chapter [4] are taken from *The Golden Ass* by Lucius Apuleius (c. A.D. 120- c. 180); they epitomize sexual prowess. The translated passages in italics are taken from *Ten Days That Shook the World* (1919) by John Reed (1887–1920); they refer to the Russian Revolution.

15. He describes himself (ironically?) to Bernard as "a failure as a bourgeois and a failure as a revolutionary" (252, 298).

16. Charles too is involved in sublimation, at least of a chemical kind, since he devotes much of his time to wine-making.

[17]Cf. "it was as if I were talking to some ghost, or perhaps to my own ghost—for perhaps he didn't speak, hadn't even any need to speak [. . .] and not two voices alternating but perhaps just one, or perhaps none" (125, 151).

18. The words *half* and *cut off f]* appear in English in the original French version of the novel.

19. On the significance of the lake motif in *Histoire,* see Sarkonak, *Claude Simon: les carrefours du texte,* pp. 132–50.

20. There is no reason to believe that Corinne has committed suicide as the dust jacket of the American edition of *Histoire* would lead one to think.

21. Jiménez-Fajardo, *Claude Simon,* p. 107.

22. Cf. Jean Starobinski, "La journée dans *Histoire*" in *Sur Claude Simon* (Paris: Minuit, 1987), pp. 7–32.

CHAPTER SIX

The Battle of Pharsalus (*La Bataille de Pharsale*)

Simon's sixth novel to be translated into English, *La Bataille de Pharsale* (1969), is both a continuation of earlier novels in the Reixach Cycle, especially though not exclusively *Histoire,* as well as an anticipation of some of his later works, such as *Orion aveugle* (1970, Blind Orion) and *Les Corps conducteurs* (1971, *Conducting Bodies*). At first reading, *The Battle of Pharsalus* may appear extremely complex because of the many different textual components that make up this novelistic puzzle. However, at the same time, some of these elements will be familiar to readers of Simon since they include characters whom the reader of earlier novels has already met, typical Simonian themes such as love and death, as well as actual scenes that recall *The Flanders Road* as well as *Histoire*. Using the collage or patchwork quilt technique, the novelist has included in his novel texts written by other writers, especially fragments from Marcel Proust's great multivolumed novel *A la recherche du temps perdu* (1913–27, *Remembrance of Things Past*), as well as descriptions of battle scenes inspired by famous paintings by artists of various periods. The battle of the title is thus a battle with words—Simon's own words as well as those of other writers who have written on the subjects of war and sexual jealousy—and another in the series of Simon's attempts to come to terms with images of the past—whether it be one's own past or that of members of one's family or that of another soldier-writer who happened to live two thousand years ago, Julius Caesar. The resulting novel is a fascinating aesthetic object, which, despite the variety of styles and techniques, is marked nonetheless by an overall unity of purpose and a textual playfulness that will long fascinate the attentive reader.

The title of Simon's 1969 novel refers to a battle fought between the armies of Caesar and Pompey in the dying days of the Roman Republic (50–45 B.C.). The battle, which was decisive in Caesar's ultimate defeat of Pompey, took place in August of the year 48 B.C. in the region of northern Greece called Thessaly. The classical reference comes initially from a section of a commentary written by Caesar, *De Bello Civile* (*Civil Wars*), extracts of which the narrator of *The Battle of Pharsalus* had to translate for his Latin homework when he was a schoolboy. The novel also contains references to other classical and modern works about the famous battle, including *Bellum civile* (sometimes called *Pharsalia*) by the Latin poet Lucan (A.D. 39–65). In addition, one recalls the Spanish Civil War in *The Palace,* not to mention other civil wars, such as the French and Russian Revolutions, which play such important parts in *Histoire* and *The Georgics.*

In French the title contains the anagram "La bataille de la phrase" (the battle of the sentence),[1] whereas in English one could also read "the battle of the phallus." Given the erotic scenes portrayed and the emphasis on stylistic experimentation in the novel,

113

both of these anagrammatic readings would be apt sub-
titles for Simon's modern version of an ancient and
eternal occupation of man, namely war, whether it be
between opposing armies or sexual partners. As is obvious from any reading of his novels, war, like sex, is
a recurring theme (cf. *The Flanders Road, The Palace,
Histoire*). Readers should not be shocked that war in
these novels is not the object of a moral debate or con-
demnation: Simon uses war as his raw material, not
just because he himself has had first-hand experience
of it, but because so many writers and artists have
written about war or painted pictures of battles. In the
case of *The Battle of Pharsalus,* readers familiar with
Simon's early work *La Corde raide* will recognize
scenes that apparently were part of the novelist's actual wartime experiences in Flanders. More important, however, readers may recognize famous paintings the writer used as points of departure for his description of the Battle of Pharsalus. These paintings
are aesthetic objects, whatever one thinks of the spectacle of men killing each other, whether in 48 B.C. on
the plains of Thessaly or in 1940 on a road in Flanders.
Finally, readers should be prepared for the fact that
the descriptions in the novel, both of battle scenes and
various sexual practices, are explicit and verge on
what some might consider crudity.

As is usual in Simon, the novel opens in medias res
and, what is more, in midflight:

Yellow and then black in the wink of an eye then
yellow again: wings outspread crossbow shape and
shot between the sun and the eye shadows for an
instant across the face like velvet like a hand for an

instant shadows then light or rather a recollection (warning?) a recall of the shadows leaping up with the speed of light palpable [. . .].[2]

The novel begins with the perception of a moving object and the problems it raises (perception precedes designation). In fact, it is only several lines later on that the word "bird" is used and the type of bird—a pigeon—is not mentioned until the second paragraph, and then only in connection with the traditional symbol of the Holy Spirit portrayed as a white dove in a stained-glass window. At the first reading, readers cannot possibly know what they are supposed to *see,* just as the narrating voice doesn't know what has been seen; all we have is a fleeting vision of colors. Which is to say that the telling of the scene is as problematical as the actual content itself. However, even at such an early stage in our reading of the novel, things begin to make some sense, for example, the yellow light associated with the sun, which is mentioned in the epigraph to the first part of the novel,[3] stands in sharp contrast to the darkness of the moving object. Yellow and black objects will be described again and again throughout the novel; here the two colors occur in rapid succession, for the time that it takes the viewer's eye to blink is just long enough for the object to disappear.

Once again Simon begins a novel with the image of a bird, this time a bird flying so fast that the viewer-narrator barely has time to see it, and certainly not the time to describe it or even to formulate the word "bird." The beginning of *The Battle of Pharsalus* recalls that of *The Palace* as well as *Histoire* for all three involve birds. Here, the bird appears as a sensory enigma: a shape and a color, but also a smell and a sound (of rustling air) as the text goes on to say. The unfolded wings recall a crossbow while the pigeon flies by the window, that is, between the viewer's face and the sun. This fleeting glimpse, or perhaps it would be more accurate to say this memory, of something black immediately leads the narrator to recall other forms of darkness—the darkness of night, the darkness of the earth, the darkness of death. While the viewer remains passively immobile, except for the blink of an eye, the bird incarnates extraordinary movement and speed, like that of an arrow shot from a crossbow. This in turn will lead to the image of battles fought before the invention of gunpowder, such as the Battle of Pharsalus. While doves are a traditional symbol for peace, it will be recalled that carrier pigeons were used to deliver messages in wartime and that feathers were used to make both quill pens and arrows. Thus, some of the major themes of the novel—life and death, mobility and immobility, writing and war—have already been put in context by these first few lines of text.

Finally, there is another binary "opposition" one should keep in mind, ancient and modern times. The former are present in the title and the first epigraph—Caesar, Zeno of Elea, Achilles—while the latter are evoked by the name of the novelist and the obvious fact that we are reading a modern text. As will become progressively more clear as readers continue through the textual landscape, Simon is deliberately recycling *old* textual material—pieces and bits not only of history, but also of his own earlier novels, such as the bird motif—in the writing of a *new* text whose form takes shape before our somewhat startled eyes.

Readers will recognize among the characters in *The Battle of Pharsalus* the grandmother from *Histoire,* as well as Uncle Charles, Van Velden, his wife, the model, and even Corinne and her brother Paulou. To be sure, some new characters have been added to the fictional cast: Nikos, a friend of the narrator who accompanies him on a car trip to Greece; and an old soldier known as the gladiator, who bunked in the same barracks as the narrator and who, because of a kind of innate pathetic grandeur, is like some modern caricature of the warriors of ancient times described by Caesar or painted by Nicolas Poussin. As for the narrating voice, it appears to be that of the narrator in *Histoire;* at the same time his wartime experiences recall those of Georges in *The Flanders Road.* In fact, while it is impossible (on the level of fictional coherence and verisimilitude) that these two narrators are one and the same "person," here, at least, parts of their stories merge in one novel, one text.

While it is true that characters from *Histoire* reappear in *The Battle of Pharsalus,* the emphasis in the 1969 novel is definitely not on their psychological makeup. Using a technique with which he experimented in his two previous novels, Simon places *The Battle of Pharsalus* under the sign of an all-encompassing ambiguity that marks the end of the Reixach Cycle. This is especially true in the last part of the novel where all of the characters merge under the single, anonymous designation of "O." While it is not always easy to divide up Simon's *oeuvre* into periods, one can situate the break between his second and third manners of writing between the second and third *parts* of *The Battle of Pharsalus.* In the last part of this novel, as in the next three novels (*Conducting Bodies, Triptych,* and *The World About Us*), characters are little more than the fictional pretexts for the staging of the writing. In these later works, the characters are developed even less than in the last part of *The Battle of Pharsalus* where they still carry a certain emotional resonance, largely due to what the reader remembers about the personalized antecedents of O. from the first two parts of the novel as well as from *Histoire.*

As to thematic content, the 1969 text reads like a replay of Simon's earlier novels. Sexual love and jealousy, war, pain, and death are some of the principal themes in *The Battle of Pharsalus.* As in the other novels of the Reixach Cycle, knowledge, or rather the difficulty and even the impossibility of our ever knowing anything for certain, is a kind of supertheme the narrative articulates not only in terms of content but also by the very example of its own writing or composition. One of the leitmotifs of the novel is the refrain "I didn't yet know," contrasting the young narrator's naïveté with what he is later to learn on the battlefield in Flanders. Although he had often read about war, notably in the passages of Caesar's *De Bello Civile* which he was supposed to translate, when he himself witnessed the real thing, it suddenly seemed entirely different:

> *I didn't yet know that expressions like walking into fire baptism by fire tasting fire were not metaphors firearms and that the traces war leaves behind are*

simply black and dirty exactly like the soot of a chimney [. . .]. (76, 111)

The effect of reality is to concretize the metaphors the adolescent had encountered in his homework assignments and which he had always interpreted to be mere figures of speech. To the surprise of the former student, language turns out to be the most evocative, the most descriptive, and the most realistic when it is metaphorical. Of course, the lesson is precisely what this and other novels by Simon demonstrate by their use of metaphor and simile.

The other supertheme can be deduced from the title of the first part of the novel, itself taken from Paul Valéry, "Achilles Running Motionless." Whether it be the odd combination of movement and immobility of the people seen exiting a subway station on an escalator or the impression the World War II soldier has of running on the spot while being shot at by the enemy, movement appears, as in the writings of the philosopher Zeno of Elea (c. 490–430 B.C.), to be a paradox that defies logic. Now Simon is not a philosopher, and the problem posed by movement interests him primarily as it affects the techniques of novel-writing and, in particular, description. In a novel, movement, like the rest of the fiction, is a question of illusion, for of course nothing moves among the black spots on the page before the reader's eyes. In a similar manner, although using different techniques and working in a different medium, the painter of a battle scene, for example, must create the effect that will lead to the viewer's imagining that the people and things portrayed have been "captured" in one instant of fictitious time. Movement is usually thought to be narrated whereas static scenes are supposed to be described. In Simon, however, the distinction between narration and description is blurred if not made totally redundant,[4] for movement is forever arrested, while immobile scenes, such as the marble frieze of horseriders described at the end of the novel, are continually animated. The passage in the novel from movement to immobility and vice versa is so subtle as to be almost invisible, which proves that what we are dealing with is a technique of writing rather than a mere theme. Like the figures of speech about war—which the narrator ends up experiencing as real during "his" war—the principal themes of the text are illustrated, exemplified, or textualized by the narrative so that the reader may experience them all the more directly. Readers of *The Battle of Pharsalus* will have the opportunity of reliving, for example, the impossibility of knowledge or movement, not just at the level of content, but also and especially through their interpretation of the narrative and stylistic devices Simon has utilized to portray and incarnate the themes of the novel. As in all great literature, this is a novel that does what it says, or rather what it writes.

Like *The Flanders Road,* the structure of *The Battle of Pharsalus* is tripartite, as in a triptych, which underscores the plastic qualities of the writing. The first and longest part of the novel, "Achilles Running Motionless," introduces the scenes to which the narrative will return. These range from the initial sequence in which a first-person narrator sees a pigeon fly by his window while he is sitting at his desk in Paris while writing or waiting to write, to memories of a recent trip to Greece during which he tried to locate the precise site of the battle of Pharsalus which he had read about as a child. The narrative is divided into paragraphs of varying length printed in roman and italic type—italics indicate remembered fragments of Uncle Charles's "speeches" in which he lectured his nephew on the necessity of acquiring linguistic skills in order to survive in today's world, as well as passages borrowed from other texts. In this part of his novel, as in earlier novels of the same period, Simon still makes use of present participles but little punctuation.

The second part of the novel, "Lexicon," is divided into seven sections, each of which has a heading very like a dictionary entry, that is, the titles are of the words as "defined" by Simon. These sections of narrative "vocabulary," arranged alphabetically in French, are as follows: Battle (made up of descriptions of famous paintings of battles[5] juxtaposed with World War II memories), Caesar (describing a visit to Lourdes in which the narrator's grandmother is identified with the figure of Julius Caesar), Conversation (describing a visit with Van Velden's wife while both the painter and his model are suspiciously absent), Gladiator (describing a drunken soldier), Machine (describing an old combine-harvester which, like some of the material in the earlier novels in the Reixach Cycle, is still being recycled for its parts although it is essentially finished, unusable as a whole),[6] Travel (describing a train journey undertaken to visit famous works of art[7] in Italy and Germany) and O. (describing a jealous man in a Paris square who looks at the window of the apartment where he suspects the model of deceiving him with Van Velden).

In the last section of the novel, "Chronology of Events,"[8] the narrative returns to the various scenes of the fiction, but with an important difference. This time the identities of the characters are erased or subsumed by the common designation "O," which can be read as both the letter (as in a geometry problem) and the number (as in the title of the well-known essay *Writing Degree Zero* [1953] by the French critic and theorist, Roland Barthes [1915–80]). At various stages in the third part of the novel, one can identify O. as any and all of the following characters:

—the train traveler

—the traveler in Italy

—the visitor to the artist's studio in company with the model

—the father of Paulou and Corinne

—the reader looking up a passage in Proust about jealousy

—the stamp collector

—the female model

—the observer looking at an antiwar demonstration in front of a barracks

—the traveler in Greece

—the schoolboy doing his Latin homework

—the French cavalryman in World War II

—the jealous man in the corridor

—the traveler in Germany

—the young companion of Paulou and Corinne when they were children

—the man in the darkened office who pays some laborers

—the person who comments critically on a text about German art written by a French art historian

—the person planning a car trip to Greece
—Nikos's friend who spends a night in Verona
—the man who visits Van Velden's studio and talks with his wife
—the jealous man looking at an apartment window
—the writer of the first sentence of the novel

While at first glance one might be tempted to say that there are not really some twenty different characters involved, one must be wary of identifying characters and attaching names to them. For example, one could say that the schoolboy and the soldier in World War II are one and the same person, that is, the narrator. However, if we go back to *The Flanders Road* and *Histoire,* it will be recalled that Georges and the narrator of the latter novel, while they share some common traits, are not identical. Furthermore, even if one does identify the schoolboy and the soldier as the narrator, or the jealous lover and the traveler in Italy as Uncle Charles, who can say that they are one and the same person? As time passes so too characters change and evolve so that it becomes problematic to identify one incarnation of O. with another: "I myself no longer the same already several hundred yards away already several seconds older" (112, 164). Furthermore, *The Battle of Pharsalus* continues to exploit the fundamental similarity between the ex-student and his Uncle Charles, which rendered so much of *Histoire* ambiguous. It is impossible to tell if the man in the cafe is Charles or his nephew, for textual evidence will support both interpretations.[9] Simon's novel puts into question not only how we construct characters—by saying that this fragment of text refers to the same person as this other segment—but also the uniqueness and the identity of human beings as they change and evolve throughout a lifetime, or what in many cases might be considered several lives, incarnations, or roles.

The style of writing changes too, for the third part of *The Battle of Pharsalus* is written in the present tense with conventional punctuation and narrated from a third-person point of view. However, as might be expected with Simon, the ordering of the events and scenes described is not chronological in any ordinary sense of the term; rather the use of the present tense tends to place all the scenes—the battle scenes of World War II as well as the cavalry charge represented on an ancient marble frieze—on the same temporal plane. Thus the chronology is more one of the writing and reading of the actual order of narrative sequences than of the events that form the "plot" of the novel. In the end, all the various elements of the fiction, which in principle range over a period of 2000 years, seem to coexist in one eternal present, as though time, like Achilles in Valéry's poem, were "running motionless" to come back to the initial epigraph of the novel.

Apart from *The Georgics,* which also incorporates a great number of different documentary sources, Simon uses the technique of intertextuality more in *The Battle of Pharsalus* than in any of his other novels to date. At the level of action, the narrative takes the form of a patchwork of old fictional material because of the presence of reappearing character names (Van Velden, Corinne, etc.), and stories the faithful reader of Simon will recognize—the World War II scenes, as well as references to the war in Spain—taken from *The Flanders Road, The Palace,* and *Histoire.* It also contains allusions to other novels that, although not actually named or identified, are nonetheless implicitly present in Simon's own novel: Michel Butor's *Change of Heart* (*La Modification,* 1957), a tale of train journeys and failed relationships; Graham Greene's *The Heart of the Matter* (1948), the illustrated cover of which is described in less than flattering terms in the Travel section of the novel; Pauline Réage's sexually explicit novel, *Story of O* (*Histoire d'O,* 1954); Alain Robbe-Grillet's *Jealousy* (*La Jalousie,* 1957) in which precise descriptions of material objects "hide" an obsessed, jealous spectator; and William Faulkner's *The Sound and the Fury* (1929) in which one name, Quentin, refers to two characters of opposite sexes. Finally, at the level of the material text, the novel contains numerous quotations from different sources—varying from commercial signs to longer passages taken, as already mentioned, from diverse literary and historical sources. Sometimes the collage technique can be discerned by the actual typography of the book, for the text contains a mixture of print styles, languages, and texts: roman and italic characters, Greek letters—lower- and upper-case—not to mention fragments in Spanish and Italian, several pictograms, and even a phonetic transcription of a passage from Proust's novel, in which jealousy plays such an important role.[10] Some of the other important writers whose texts enter into this intertextual collage are Caesar (*Civil Wars*), Apuleius (*The Golden Ass*), and Elie Faure (*History of Art*). Although it would be a difficult challenge for a reader to isolate and identify all the sources of the text, it is more important to understand how Simon's technique of intertextuality works to make one coherent whole out of a variety of sources. In fact, the textual mortar that is used to hold the many scenes and sequences together is often so invisible that readers may not be aware that they are passing from a passage written by Simon to one quoted from another writer. The fact that Simon chooses to include passages from other texts is not only an implicit homage to other writers, which it is especially in the case of Proust, for the passages also function quite simply as part and parcel of Simon's raw materials—like the letters and words we all recycle when we write—which he then reworks by integrating them into the specific context of his narrative.

There are numerous passages which exploit the technique of textual collage; one will suffice to illustrate the process:

> come on let's get this over with otherwise we won't be eating until nine o'clock sometimes you could think about how much you're hurting your mother write A *river* with steep banks protected his right wing
>
> Do you see something that looks like a *river*? (33, 53) [Emphasis added; trans. alt.]

The first paragraph belongs to the series of scenes describing the narrator's youth: Charles is berating his nephew for wasting time at the local fair instead of doing his Latin homework. Anxious to eat dinner, Charles gives the narrator the correct answer, the French translation of Caesar's commentary describing the site of the Battle of Pharsalus, the actual wording of which appeared on the previous page, "*dextrum cornu ejus rivus quidam impeditis ripis muniebat*" (A river with steep banks protected his right wing).[11] On the other hand, the second paragraph belongs to the journey to Greece when the narrator and his friend Nikos attempt to find the river mentioned in the sentence that the schoolboy was unable to translate correctly. The novel is playing here with words and things and how the link between the two may change in importance for us as we grow older. Significantly, the textual source in the first paragraph is totally integrated into the context, which emphasizes how easily memories and actual perceptions, past and present, as well as books and reality can be made to coalesce in a new text. Clearly, one cannot accuse Simon of lacking originality any more than one would accuse artists such as Marcel Duchamp (1887–1968) or Robert Rauschenberg (1925–   ) of doing so when they make use of already existing objects in their works of art. What is important is the manner in which the old material, whether text or object, has been fashioned into a new aesthetic object.

It is therefore not surprising for a technique that plays such a significant part in the novel's composition to be thematicized within it. As is so often the case, Simon's novels provide their own commentary in the form of scale models or mirrors inserted into his fiction, particularly since *The Grass*. In this regard, *The Battle of Pharsalus* is no exception, for the collage technique is itself described and illustrated in passages such as the following extract: "[. . .] man and nature being, in the enormous landscape now revealed, closely identified and, one might say, belonging to one and the same kingdom in which animal vegetable and mineral are amalgamated [. . .]" (77, 112–13). Here, rather than mere intertextuality, we are dealing with a pictorial source, since the passage can be related to Pieter Breughel's painting, *Battle of Gelboe with the Suicide of Saul* (1562). However, just as Simon's textual sources are recontextualized, rewritten, in *The Battle of Pharsalus,* so too the descriptions based on famous paintings are totally integrated into the novel. In this case, the scene described, the intermingling of man and nature, also represents the intermingling of the various textual materials and narrative strands as much as a battle in ancient times.

The Battle of Pharsalus is best thought of as a type of collage whose significance is furnished by the very unity of its structure. In the Simonian view of the world, there is no permanence, only a permanent state of flux. All "things"—human beings and the ordinary as well as the cultural objects they create and live with—are subject to destruction and disintegration (the pair of frightened lovers transformed into a painting and then a sculpture which ends up falling to pieces). *Homo significans,* mankind as an animal who produces *meaning,* is forever dissatisfied with the existing order of things, including his own very obvious mortality. In the face of universal entropy all we can do is to create new objects, which of course are destined eventually to be reintegrated into new ensembles, just as fragments of Proust's novel are incorporated into Simon's novel. This inexorable tendency for all structures to be absorbed into a new order is illustrated vividly by one of the most transitory of all structures, the bubbles in an ordinary bottle of beer. "The sun gleamed on the translucent walls of the bubbles Now and then *one of them exploded the group of translucent cells immediately reorganizing into another structure* meshes of a net in all directions" (114, 167–68 [emphasis added]). Simon's 1969 novel is formed with bits and pieces of the past—experiences, memories, perceptions—all of which have been "reorganiz[ed] into another structure." Of course, this textual play with words and texts, with images and works of art is no more gratuitous than the productions of any artist. And as such the reorganized mesh of this novel itself can only be transitory.

The difference between *Histoire,* in which Simon recycled memorabilia from his own family's past, and *The Battle of Pharsalus* is that in the later novel he makes greater use of historical, artistic, and literary mementoes that are part of the public domain, part of the cultural background and heritage of a contemporary Everyman. Moreover, whereas in *Histoire* the collage technique can often (though not always) be justified in terms of mnemonic associations, in *The Battle of Pharsalus* the stylistic and narrative structures of the novel are more often based on a purely verbal logic. One cannot say that either of the two novels is better since both of them are successful in what they set out to do. However, *Histoire* is somewhat more accessible to those who read Simon in translation since some of the linguistic playfulness of *The Battle of Pharsalus* is necessarily lost in the English-language version. Given the greater emphasis on the subversion of character portrayal and the different writing styles used in the 1969 novel, it is very definitely a transitional text, a kind of provisional structure in the evolution of the art of the novel as practiced by Simon. *The Battle of Pharsalus* not only casts a nostalgic glance toward the past—that of Europe as well as that of the Reixach

129

Cycle—but also anticipates the later novels. The novelist inaugurated his third style or manner of writing with a change in his novelistic personnel as well as a change in the fictional locale since in his next novel, *Conducting Bodies,* both the Reixach clan and Europe are abandoned, at least for the duration of what one might call Simon's American holiday.

NOTES

1. Cf. Ricardou, "La Bataille de la phrase" in *Pour une théorie du nouveau roman,* pp. 118–58.

2. *The Battle of Pharsalus,* trans. Richard Howard (New York: Braziller, 1971), p. 3; *La Bataille de Pharsale* (Paris: Minuit, 1969), p. 9. Subsequent references will appear in parentheses in the text.

3.   *Zénon! Cruel Zénon! Zénon d'Elée!*
    M'as-tu percé de cette flèche ailée
    Qui vibre, vole, et qui ne vole pas!
    Le son m'enfante et la flèche me tue!
    Ah! le soleil . . . Quelle ombre de tortue
    Pour l'âme, Achille immobile à grands pas!

    Zeno, cruel Zeno, Eleatic Zeno,
    Your winged arrow finds its mark
    And flying sings, and does not fly!
    The sound is birth, the arrow death,
    And the sun . . . A tortoise shadow for
    The soul, Achilles running motionless.

From "Le Cimetière marin" (1920) by Paul Valéry (1871–1945); this is the version that appears in Richard Howard's translation of the novel.

4. Cf. "In fact, by animating images they are turned into stories; in other words, description is 'narrativized'" (Jean Rousset, "La guerre en peinture," *Critique* 414 [1981]: 1207 [my trans.]).

5. For readers interested in art who wish to compare Simon's

luxuriant prose to the original pictorial sources or "stimulants," the paintings are as follows: Piero della Francesca (1416–92), *The Battle Between Heraclius and Chosroes* (1460: fresco *The Legend of the True Cross,* Church of St. Francesco, Arezzo): 69–72, 101–05; detail, 186, 268–70 (cf. drawing by Claude Simon in *Orion aveugle*); Paolo Uccello (1397–1475), *Unhorsing of Bernardino della Carda,* panel from the triptych *The Battle of San Romano* (1455: [The painting described was originally the central panel which portrayed the last stage of the battle.] Uffizi, Florence): 72–75, 105–10; Pieter Breughel (the Elder) (c. 1525–69), *Battle of Gelboe with the Suicide of Saul* (1562: Kunsthistorisches Museum, Vienna): 76–78, 112–15; Nicolas Poussin (1594–1665), *The Victory of Joshua over the Amorites* (1625–26: Pushkin Museum of Fine Arts, Moscow): 79–81, 116–19 and later on 139, 200–01 as well as 167–68, 241–42.

6. "As it stands, the machine is evidently incomplete; several of its parts are missing" (102, 149).

7. The paintings used in this section are Nicolas Poussin, *Landscape with Blind Orion* (1658: Metropolitan Museum of Art, New York): (111, 162–63), which will play such an important role in *Orion aveugle* and *Les Corps conducteurs;* Alphonse de Neuville (1835–85), *The Last Cartridges* (1873: private collection): 113–14, 166–68. The latter is in the so-called realist style, on an artistic level with the novel described in the same section.

8. The paintings used in this section are Jacques Louis David (1748–1825), *The Rape of the Sabines* (1799: Musée du Louvre, Paris): 135–36, 194–95 (The detail of Medusa's head at the center of the soldier's shield—so appropriate in a novel that explores the theme of petrification—is borrowed from an Italian bank note.); Lucas Cranach (the Elder) (1472–1553): *The Close of the Silver Age* [sometimes called *Jealousy* or *The Effects of Jealousy*] (c. 1530: National Gallery, London): 156–58, 226–28.

9. The traveler in Italy appears to be Charles since he sends a postcard to his children, Corinne and Paulou, after writing and then destroying a letter he was going to send to a woman (Van Velden's model?). At the same time, the man looking so intently, so obsessively at a particular apartment window (where he suspects the model of deceiving him with Van Velden?) while sitting on the terrace of a Parisian cafe cannot possibly be Charles, for a newspaper headline situates that particular human drama in 1968 at the time

of student unrest on the suburban university campus of Nanterre. Given the difference in their ages, these two incarnations of O. cannot be either Charles or his nephew. In the final analysis, the jealous lover is irrevocably ambiguous for he is neither Charles nor his younger nephew, or, to put it more accurately, as in life, there are more actors than characters here. O. is the jealous lover, in the same way that an actor plays a part in a well-known play that has been staged many times over the years.

10. See Françoise Van Rossum-Guyon's article, "De Claude Simon à Proust: un exemple d'intertextualité," *Lettres Nouvelles* 4 (Sept.–Oct. 1972): 107–37.

11. *De Bello Civile,* 3.88.

CHAPTER SEVEN

Conducting Bodies
(*Les Corps conducteurs*)

Les Corps conducteurs (1971) is the first novel that belongs entirely to the third manner of Simon's writing,
although the last part of *The Battle of Pharsalus* did
inaugurate a definite break with the other novels of
the Reixach Cycle. *Conducting Bodies*, the first of
three relatively short novels published in the 1970s
which include *Triptyque* (1973) and *Leçon de choses*
(1975, *The World About Us*), completes that rupture
with Simon's earlier style. Although *Conducting Bodies* is not as successful as Simon's two subsequent novels, it constitutes a unique case both as to its genesis
and thematics. The time frame of the narrative ranges
from the fifteenth century to the 1960s; the fiction
takes place chiefly in a large North American metropolis and a South American country where a writers'
conference is held; and among the themes developed
by Simon in his new style of writing are the functions
and disfunctions of the human body, the commercial
and sexual exploitation of the individual, as well as a
biting satire about a certain conception of literature
that Simon does not share.

The genesis of *Conducting Bodies*[1] was unlike any
other of the novels written by Simon up until that
time. Originally he was invited by the Swiss publish-

ing house Editions Albert Skira to write a book in its series, "Les sentiers de la création" (Paths of Creation), in which other writers, such as Michel Butor and Roland Barthes, also participated.[2] *Orion aveugle* (Blind Orion) was the result, a beautifully designed book of 145 pages, including a drawing by Simon himself, a facsimile handwritten 10-page preface, 20 illustrations including reproductions of works by the American artists Robert Rauschenberg (1925-) and Louise Nevelson (1900–88), and an accompanying fictional text by the author.[3] Later, Simon continued to work on the textual portion of the art book which grew into a novel published by his regular publisher in Paris, Les Editions de Minuit, under a new title, *Les Corps conducteurs,* without either the art reproductions or the preface that had accompanied the earlier book. (This was not the first time Simon had worked with visual stimuli: he made use of postcards in *Histoire* and famous paintings in *The Battle of Pharsalus,* including the magnificent *Landscape with Blind Orion* [1658] by Nicolas Poussin [1594–1665], which is reproduced in the art book to which it gave its name.)[4]

The title suggests conductors through which heat or electricity can be induced to flow. Furthermore, the human body, its anatomy and sicknesses will be a major theme of the novel. However, other kinds of bodies are also described, such as animal and celestial bodies (stars) which in turn are often based on mythological characters, as well as bodies represented figuratively (drawings, paintings, sculptures) and verbally. In some cases, the notion of the body undergoes a certain blurring as in the case of Blind Orion who is at once a mythological character, a constellation seen in the southern sky, and a famous painting by Poussin. As is so often the case with Simon's titles, this one can be read at more than one level: on the one hand, a physical, realistic level and on the other, a metaphorical and symbolical level, for the bodies in question are represented by words, not images, in the novel. The path along which the current flows could be compared to the narrative thread which allows readers to make their way through the mass of words that make up the text. These words convey the meaning of the novel and may even give rise to the occasional shock.

While it would not be entirely accurate to say that there are no characters whatsoever in *Conducting Bodies,* character definitely plays a reduced role even when compared to *The Battle of Pharsalus,* for example. As in the other novels of Simon's third manner, the emphasis is squarely on the description of visual elements. Relationships, including those between human beings in close proximity, are described in purely spatial terms. Just as a modern painter sets himself the challenge of juxtaposing various shapes and colors in an abstract painting, so too at this stage in Simon's career, the problems of narrative and textual continuity preoccupied him far more than even the fragmentary and partial representation of characters which one finds in the volumes of the Reixach Cycle, let alone the traditional portrayal of character in conventional narrative.

Conducting Bodies is as streamlined a novel as one could imagine: it contains no subtitle or epigraph. Moreover, the text of the narrative takes the form of a single textual block without any division into parts, chapters, or even paragraphs. On the other hand, tra-

135

ditional punctuation is respected and the novel is narrated in the present tense from the point of view of an anonymous third person, stylistic features of the last part of Simon's previous novel. Against this backdrop of textual continuity, it is possible to discern a number of different fictional series: a sick man wanders through a large North American city, which though unnamed certainly suggests New York; Blind Orion stumbles toward the horizon; a traveler takes a plane to South America; a foreign participant attends a conference on the political role of the modern writer; a group of explorers attempts to make its way through the jungles of South America; and a man is rejected by a woman whom he loves. While one might be tempted to identify the traveler in the plane, the sick man in the street, and the rejected lover as one and the same person, this is not necessarily the case. Nevertheless, the novel is unified to the extent that each series affects the reader's interpretation of all the others.[5] For example, the traveler recalls other travelers, notably the sixteenth-century explorers of South America as well as Blind Orion who is heading toward an unseen destination. Further unity is provided at the thematic level of the narrative: the writers' conference is a failure; the explorers' expedition is doomed to failure as one by one the soldiers fall victim to illness and die; the night of love-making appears destined never to happen again; the traveler is tired and sick.

The image of America[6] which the reader is left with after reading *Conducting Bodies* is one of variety and contrast, just as the narrative itself is made up of a large number of juxtaposed heterogeneous parts and fragments. Perhaps the most significant characteristic of Simon's New World is its huge size, for everything—the rivers, the mountains, the jungles, the geographical distances between cities, the cities, and the buildings in the cities—is as gigantic as Orion himself. (Appropriately enough, Poussin's painting is part of the giant art collection of the Metropolitan Museum of New York.) Commercialism dominates the urban landscape and permeates every area of human endeavor, including religion. As for the environment, it is distinctly dangerous. The heat and humidity of both the urban and tropical jungles prove to be uncomfortable and downright harmful to the health of the human beings portrayed; the noises in the streets and the subway assault the sick man. Violence and death loom in the not-so-distant background: photos of the assassination of John Kennedy; the well-oiled guns of policemen seen in an airport; the strange (and perhaps violent?) people observed in the streets; the invisible parasites of the South American jungle which invade the orifices of the soldiers' bodies, causing them unbearable pain and hallucinations before they die, grotesquely deformed from mysterious diseases.

This leads to the most significant characteristic of Simon's America: the alienation experienced by the individual who ends up emptied of his or her subjectivity and identity. Some readers may find *Conducting Bodies* heavy going, and it is true that at times the novel may appear as cold and clinical as anatomical drawings. But one should keep in mind that this impersonal style of writing is part and parcel of the sense of alienation that pervades the entire narrative. For example, both spatially and temporally the individual feels crushed by the impersonal environment. It is not by chance that time is described metaphorically as an avalanche of foreign material which nothing can make recede.[7] Language itself contributes to the sense of alienation the traveler experiences. The delegates to the conference talk endlessly in the smoke-filled backrooms of the Chamber of Deputies; the cityscape of the North American metropolis is covered with verbal messages inciting the passersby to find God, shop at certain stores, take courses to improve themselves, or try their luck at the state lottery. Within the space of the novel, a multitude of typographical images in bold-face capitals embedded in the pages of continuous prose jump out at the reader just as the ever-present signs, advertisements, and graffiti of the urban environment attack the city dwellers. The proliferation of foreign (English) words used to force the individual to undertake some action which other persons wish him or her to perform for whatever reason, makes language—our principal way of creating meaning in a chaotic world—into a formidable alien power that seeks to govern our every move and action.

As to interpersonal contact, Simon describes again and again the expressionless faces, the averted eyes of all those with whom the traveler comes in contact. Even love leads nowhere as in the early morning sunlight, the woman and the man face not so much each other as the impossibility of continuing their relationship after a night of passionate love-making. Speaking intimately to another human being demands an extraordinary effort, which is to no avail in any case.[8] Finally, men and women find themselves alienated from that most intimate part of themselves, their own bodies. The forced smiles and the contorted positions of the models shown displaying their genitalia on the covers of magazines in the window of a sex boutique speak eloquently of the commercial exploitation of sex. Finally, of course, there are bodily disfunctions. The traveler is so sick that even the most simple of activities, such as walking or sitting, have become difficult, sometimes impossible. Pain, which comes and goes in excruciating spasms, separates and alienates him from his own body, leaving him at the end of the novel a solitary, broken man lying face down on a dirty and threadbare carpet in an anonymous hotel room.[9]

What then should be the social and political function of the writer in such an alienating world? Simon eschews directly anwering this highly polemical question. But he does include ideas of the opposing camp who believe, like Jean-Paul Sartre, in a literature that is committed to specific causes (*littérature engagée*), namely one whose principal function is to express a socially and politically "correct" message.[10] The speech-making and the political stances taken by the delegates to the writers' and politicians' conference are reported both in Spanish and a simultaneous translation, which accompanies the "original" text:

¡Me parece que (In my opinion) la única jerarquía posible (the only hierarchy that merits discussion) es la jerarquía (is the hierarchy) de los problemas y de las necesidades (of the problems and the needs) de los pueblos de nuestros países (of the peoples of our countries), y ninguna otra! (and no other) ¡Me parece que si estamos reunidos aquí (It is my opinion that if we have gathered together here), es para discutir de esos problemas (it is to discuss these problems) y no de los problemas académicos (and not theoretical problems) de una creación literaria (of literary creation) con los cuales nuestros pueblos oprimidos (which to our oppressed peoples) no tienen nada que hacer! (are of no concern whatsoever!). (50, 62–63)

Inserted into the pages of descriptive prose of *Conducting Bodies,* these speeches form an odd and vivid contrast with the rest of the text. As is usual in Simon, spoken discourse is characterized by a prosaic style, the unoriginality of the thoughts expressed and the ultimate ineptitude of the message, whatever "good" intentions may have motivated the speaker. A clue to the satirical dimension of this part of the novel is the dry, abstract, and repetitive nature of the messages. Whereas recurring descriptive scenes occur in Simon with a meaningful difference, texts such as the one quoted above are always already redundant.

Of course, Simon's point is not that nothing can be done for or that no one should speak about oppressed peoples. For Simon all he can do legitimately within the scope and space of a novel is what he is competent to do, which is to remain faithful to his own aesthetic criteria. Hence the answer to the objection about theoretical problems is furnished by the text itself: Its very existence and unique composition are ample proof that writing is not an academic problem which does not concern most people. Rather, the ability to produce works of art meets one of the most fundamental of all human needs—the drive to produce, to create, to make something beautiful that can stand on its own. The political, socio-economic, and artistic freedom to *make* things is no doubt one of the most important of humanity's inalienable rights, and unfortunately it is probably the instinctual drive least respected in today's consumer society. The writer—as this novel aptly demonstrates—does deal with the "real world," the very real world of words. These words conjure up images of reality in the mind's eye of the reader, and it is the primary task of the writer to make sure that the words he uses make sense, that they fit together properly just as engineers' constructions—bridges, roads, tunnels— must hold up if they are to function properly. This view of literature is not a trivialization of artistic endeavors; rather it is an acknowledgment of the specificity and unique character of the writer's craft: to make finely wrought verbal artifacts or "poems." For Simon, these are the only true "paths of creation."[11] In other words, *Conducting Bodies* is a statement about the way Simon views his work as a writer, an implicit literary manifesto that must be deduced from the actual writing of the novel. Hence an apparent paradox inherent in Simon's practice of the novel. It is only by giving up on the facile generalizations about the social role of writers that they can remain true, not just to themselves and their art, but also to the body politic.

What is left then? Is the book totally negative? While it might be tempting for readers to think so as they make their way through the trials and tribulations of *Conducting Bodies,* such a conclusion would be erroneous since it is supported by only part of the textual evidence, the thematic content of the novel. One must bear in mind that we are dealing with a piece of literature, and whatever the story or stories told, the ultimate criterion must be the writing, just as the quality of drawing, brushstroke, and color, not the subject matter, is the basis for judging a painting. It is true that in *Conducting Bodies* human beings are portrayed as objects, for they have been dispossessed of their essential subjectivity. The only subject left intact is the subject of the writing, the subject who writes the text and organizes the jumble of material involved into a cohesive whole.[12]

In fact, Simon's solidarity with the oppressed peoples of the world is manifested in this very novel. *Conducting Bodies* is a book not just about various types of exploitation, alienation, and oppression but one in which the alienation has been *textualized,* incorporated into the actual writing of the book. It would not be an exaggeration to say that *Conducting Bodies* is a novel that "succeeds" in causing a certain amount of discomfort on the part of its readers, which is to say that the novel is not a failure. This is a novel about a search undertaken in writing, and the quest is more important than the actual goal. One recalls Blind Orion's impossible journey as he advances through the painted landscape and the night sky, as well as Achilles "running motionless," to quote the epigraph from the first part of *The Battle of Pharsalus*. Of course, it is not by chance that the earlier version of *Conducting Bodies* was named after a painting, for in the end this is what remains: not the story of a somewhat less than brilliant literary debate or a night of passionate love, but rather these pages of fine, sober prose.

NOTES

1. *Conducting Bodies,* trans. Helen Lane (London: Calder, 1975); *Les Corps conducteurs* (Paris: Minuit, 1971). References will appear in the text.

2. Michel Butor, *Les Mots dans la peinture* (1969); Roland Barthes, *L'Empire des signes* (1970).

3. Claude Simon, *Orion aveugle,* Les Sentiers de la Création series (Geneva: Skira, 1970).

4. Cf. "In the legend of Orion, the hero, blinded by the son of Dionysus, whose daughter he has violated, carries off the fire god's apprentice to help him find the dawn and restore his sight. He is later attacked by a scorpion and then killed by Artemis, who has been tricked into believing that he has seduced one of her priestesses. Artemis then sets Orion among the stars, to be eternally pursued by the Scorpion" (Loubère, *The Novels of Claude Simon,* p. 191). The full title of Poussin's painting is *Blind Orion Walking Towards the Light of the Rising Sun.* On the Orion motif in Simon, see Celia Britton, *Claude Simon: Writing the Visible,* pp. 56–60.

5. On the "failure" of *Conducting Bodies* to prevent an interpretation in which the traveler is seen as the "central character" of the novel, see Carroll's *The Subject in Question,* p. 188.

6. America here refers to both North and South America, or at least to those parts described. Of course, readers of Simon's earlier novels will not need reminding that his America is as much a fictional construct as, say, the grand hotel in *The Palace* or the battle field in *The Battle of Pharsalus.*

7. Cf. "The grayish, lumpy mass has spread farther and farther past the door and has now reached the middle of the room. A number of successive layers have fallen away from its face, so that it no longer resembles a steep cliff and now looks like an inclined plane, a sort of enormous wedge that continues to slide imperceptibly forward [. . .]" (74, 91).

8. It is by no means certain, as the back cover of the English edition of *Conducting Bodies* would have the reader believe, that the reason the lovers cannot see each other again is because of the woman's family responsibilities; such a reading is both antifeminist and reductionist. Simon simply does not give the cause for their

disunion which is presented as an unknown (and no doubt unknowable) *fait accompli.*

9. The traveler is suffering from violent bouts of nausea caused by liver disease. Now, *crise de foie* (lit., "crisis of the liver" in French) can be read as a pun for "crisis of faith." Moreover, the faith in question can be read as both faith in conventional literature (cf. the conference on the social function of the writer) *and* in the conventional ideals upon which most countries of America were founded (cf. the allegorical paintings depicting Virtue, Law, Justice, and Work which decorate the Chamber of Deputies where the conference is held).

10. See Sartre's *Qu'est-ce que la littérature?* (Paris: Gallimard, 1948) and *Les Mots* (Paris: Gallimard, 1964); see Simon's response to Sartre's position in the contemporaneous debate about the value of literature, "Pour qui donc écrit Sartre?," *L'Express* (May 28, 1964): 32–33; as well as Simon's speech to the Swedish Academy on the occasion of receiving the Nobel Prize in 1985 (*Discours de Stockholm,* pp. 14–15). See also Alastair Duncan, "Simon and Sartre," *The Review of Contemporary Fiction* 5.1 (1985): 90–95.

11. Cf. "For my part I do not know of any paths of creation other than those that are opened up step by step, i.e. word by word, through the actual process (*cheminement*) of writing" (Claude Simon, untitled preface to *Orion aveugle,* p. [6] [my trans.].

12. For a detailed reading of the various stylistic and narrative techniques used by Simon to give *Conducting Bodies* its textual cohesion, see Jean-Claude Raillon, "Eléments d'une physique littérale," *Degrés* 1.4 (1973): g1-g29.

CHAPTER EIGHT

Triptych
(*Triptyque*)

Triptyque (1973) is the second novel in the untitled trilogy of texts dating from the early 1970s that illustrate Simon's increasing preoccupation with description as the fundamental key to fiction-writing. *Triptych* represents another step in Simon's ongoing search to write intertwined stories in such a way that the colors and shapes of objects, as well as human and animal bodies, described in each narrative series constantly recall those of the other series. In *Conducting Bodies,* this technique of textual correspondences is already in place, although the fact that the sick traveler can be associated with the various story lines provides the novel with a certain ready-made unity. The challenge that Simon set himself in subsequent novels was to achieve an overall unity of effect without using a particular character as a fictional anchor.[1]

While some readers of Simon's earlier narratives may be disappointed initially by what could appear to be an obsession with technique in *Triptych,* there is no doubt that it represents an artistic *tour de force.* The novel contains descriptions of natural phenomena and human beings that are as rich in beauty as the finest poetry in the language. In fact, the novel is probably best appreciated as a prose poem, for language, with its infinite capacity for verbal resonances, distinctive rhythms, and erotic overtones, is the principal character. The actual human beings portrayed are in fact no more important than other animate or even inanimate objects described, whether it be a trout swimming in a stream that winds its way through a village or the façades of sunlit buildings in some seaside resort on the Riviera or a rain-drenched alley outside a movie theater in some industrial town in Northern France. Nevertheless, human characters do appear and the novel does tell a story, or rather stories, about them. However, *Triptych* is above all a "language feast" to be appreciated and savored for its myriad of poetic details.

The title refers to a work of art, for example, a painting consisting of three parts. Although only one of the panels of the famous *Battle of San Romano* by Paolo Uccello was used as a pictorial stimulus in *The Battle of Pharsalus,* that famous painting is in fact a triptych. One also thinks of the comic strip described in the same novel which takes the form of a triptych.[2] In terms of modern painting, Simon has a definite interest in the triptychs of the English painter, Francis Bacon (1909-), which he saw while he was in the process of working on *Triptych*.[3] Not only does the title contain an allusion to painting, and thereby a clue to the importance of description in this novel, but it also informs the reader about the structure of the novel. Appropriately enough, *Triptych* represents the writer's *third* attempt at a *tripartite* structure (cf. *The Flanders Road* and *The Battle of Pharsalus*). More important perhaps are the connotations of such a ternary form, for it evokes the Trinity, the three unities of classical

drama, Dante's use of *terza rima* in the *Divine Comedy,*
and the three parts of the traditional French school
essay known as the *dissertation.* A close analysis of the
text will reveal that in his own distinctive manner
Simon alludes to all these ternary structures in his
novel. However, whereas the structures mentioned
above are of an elevated nature, Simon refers explicitly to three of the most fundamental of ternary structures: geometrical triangles, sexual triangles, and the
triptych, a painting in which three panels are "simply"
juxtaposed.

Now, one would normally expect a novel entitled
Triptych to consist of three stories which would presumably be told or narrated in turn. Furthermore,
each part or panel of the triptych would presumably
have its own title. (One thinks of *Trois contes* [1877]
by Gustave Flaubert [1821–80].) In *The Flanders Road,*
the three parts of the novel were numbered; although
there were no titles to the individual sections of the
text, each began with an important epigraph. In *The
Battle of Pharsalus,* each part came complete with a
number, title, and its own epigraph. On the other
hand, the parts in *Triptych* are neither numbered nor
titled, and there are no epigraphs. Of course, there is
a good reason for this as will soon become evident to
readers of the novel. Although the text is divided into
three parts, the middle one of which is the longest, the
parts do not correspond to the three story lines. In fact,
each "panel" of *Triptych* presents parts of all three of
the fictional "sets," for the emphasis is on simultaneity and continuity rather than on succession.[4]

Clearly, Simon is experimenting with the triptych
form, for the various sets overlap. Any reading that

attempts to impose a traditional order upon the three stories will be doomed to failure, just as the attempts of the two boys fail when they try to arrange fragments of film strip in a would-be chronological order that turns out to be highly problematic and, in the final analysis, arbitrary. Thus one cannot assume necessarily that a story fragment in the third part "happens" after previous fragments from the same story line in the first two parts of the novel. The logic of *Triptych* is resolutely verbal, or better still, descriptive. As in the last part of *The Battle of Pharsalus,* Simon has opted for a form of writing in which the only true form of chronology is that of the actual reading of the novel. Thus the order and the "naming" of the series in the following list is purely for the reader's convenience; it is as arbitrary as the manner in which a student of geometry assigns the letters A, B, and C to the three corners of a triangle. Given the self-reflexivity of the Simonian novel, it is hardly surprising that just such a scene is in fact described in *Triptych.*

A. One series takes place in the south of France in a Mediterranean seaside resort. A middle-aged woman tries to get her son released from police custody, for he seems to have been involved in selling drugs. One of the people she seeks help from is a member of the National Assembly who turns out to be Lambert, the boyhood friend of the narrator of *Histoire* and no doubt the most unlikable of all Simon's characters. The woman herself is an older Corinne than the one we last met in the Reixach Cycle.

B. Another of the narrative series is set in a village in central France. A boy interrupts his geometry homework to engage in various forbidden games. Some boys go fishing for trout and spy on a couple copulating in a barn. The barn is also used as a rural theater in which a movie is projected. A circus number involving a clown and some puns is also a part of this series. The clown is no doubt a double of that other inveterate punster, Simon the writer. A young woman confides the care of a little girl to some children so that she can meet her lover. The children abandon the little girl and a nighttime search party is organized to find the missing girl.

C. In another story, in a northern industrial town, a young couple's marriage gets off to a disastrous start as the bridegroom abandons his bride to make love to one of his former girlfriends in a blind alley outside of a movie theater.

In all three stories, there is an element of catastrophe. In A the naked woman's son has been arrested for drug-dealing, and she is taken advantage of sexually by an unfeeling politician; in B the little girl appears to have drowned; in C the bridegroom is sick, drunk, and unfaithful on the first night of his marriage. Furthermore, the disasters are provoked by the sexual relations of some of the characters. All three catastrophes have to be pieced together so that they are like puzzles to a certain extent. But these are no ordinary puzzles since some of the pieces are missing, including the scene of the young girl's drowning. The reader of Simon's novels will be reminded of earlier novels such as *Histoire* where the central drama was also missing. Despite the comparison which has been made between the French New Novel and the detective story, Simon's novels are not like the latter really, for they provide the reader at once with too few *and* too many clues.

In all of Simon's work, colors play a significant part in the thematics and composition of his novels. In *Triptych,* they take on added significance and an enhanced potency, given the emphasis on description. Simon has characterized himself as a failed artist.[5] Nevertheless, the evidence would seem to prove him wrong, for here as elsewhere he uses his artist's palette very effectively. The only difference is that the colors are verbal, for they function in a textual rather than a visual manner. Since the hamlet described in series B recalls the village in the Jura described at the beginning of *Le Rouge et le Noir* by Stendhal, it is perhaps not surprising that the two colors that dominate the entire novel are red and black.[6] Moreover, these colors are found in many of Francis Bacon's paintings, which seem to have inspired some of the descriptions in the novel. In particular, the naked body of the actress in A, the body of a dead rabbit in B, and the body of the bedraggled bridegroom who returns to his bride in C—all more or less recall the flayed nudes of Bacon's paintings. In the context of *Triptych,* red and black are associated with blood in both a liquid and dry state.

> Either because the enthusiasm of the painter was captured principally by the body [of the actress], or because he suddenly abandoned his canvas, he has neglected to overlay the face with pigment, and hence it appears as a blood-colored mass in which the bony structure and the jaws stand out and the bared teeth gleam.[7]

> In the semidarkness enveloping more and more of the kitchen, and in contrast with the white cloth, the

bloody flesh of the head [of the rabbit] is so dark a
red that it is almost black. (113, 150)

As [the bridegroom] comes forward into the light, his
wan face seems to grow paler still, at the same time
taking on a greenish tinge which makes the trickles
of dried blood on it appear almost black. (141, 186)

In fact, the colors red and black occur with uncanny
frequency throughout the entire text, and usually one
is not far from the other, as though they had the capacity to generate each other. The repetition of the same
colors allows scenes belonging to different fictional
sets to be juxtaposed, since colors fulfill a unifying
function in the novel. Hence, one of the most profitable
ways to read this novel is to analyze not only the colors
but the configurations and patterns of colors. Such a
chromatic reading cannot fail to produce interesting
results. In the case of *Triptych,* it is safe to assume
that a color name has not been used by chance or because "that is the way it was" in this most textual of
novels!

As in many of Simon's works, eroticism and death
are the dominant themes. Eroticism here carries with
it none of the pleasure of forbidden fruit. Rather everything in the descriptions of copulating couples reminds
the reader of the impersonal world of nature of which
they form a part. When taken out of context, some of
the erotic passages might seem crude. However, when
read in the particular section of the novel where they
occur, these descriptions have nothing pornographic
about them. In fact, they are no more inherently sexual than Simon's description of a shunting engine
working in a freight yard, which needless to say has

strong erotic overtones. As to death, it appears to be as closely related to eroticism as red is to black. Death is not so much opposed to life as juxtaposed with it, for life and death are made to coexist, even to cohabit intimately, in the fictional space of *Triptych*. In terms of the characters in the novel, death is most closely associated with the disturbing figure of an old dog-faced woman, who first appeared in Simon's untranslated novel, *Le Tricheur* (1945, The Cheat).[8]

The old woman appears to be a modern version of Hecate, a Greek goddess associated with black magic and sorcery, who haunted graveyards and was able to conjure up dreams and the spirits of the dead. Sacrifices to Hecate took the form of a fish, which may relate to the fishing expedition of the schoolboys, who may have been indirectly responsible for the death by drowning of the little girl who had been entrusted to their care. The wizened body of the old woman recalls that of Marie in *The Grass,* and Hecate was often confused with Artemis, one of Marie's names. Hecate is also associated with the mother figure. The fact that the old woman is often seen cutting grass which she then transports in an old baby carriage leads one to recall the figure of the mother in *Histoire,* who, it will be recalled, was associated with a knife blade. It is certainly not by chance that *Triptych* contains so many allusions to potentially dangerous places or objects: a sawmill, a scythe, various knives, the vicious nail-filled mouth in the clown's gag which threatens to bite his leg off, and a pair of hammers (in French) or nutcrackers (in English). Nor is it by chance that the old woman raises rabbits and that Simon has included a vivid description of her blinding, bleeding, and skinning one of the animals.[9] In French, the word for rabbit is *lapin,* a word which closely resembles *la pine,* a colloquial term for the penis, so that the killing of the rabbit becomes a highly symbolic act.[10] This also leads the reader back to Simon's 1967 novel, for in both *Histoire* and *Triptyque,* a female has disappeared and is probably dead (Hélène and the little girl), and in both cases a male (Hélène's husband and one of the schoolboys) seems to feel guilt about what has happened. In both novels, male characters are made to suffer: the narrator in *Histoire* feels cut off from life, love, and happiness; and in *Triptych* the schoolboy cuts his finger rather badly. It is therefore hardly surprising that in this novel the sex act itself is textually associated with knives as well as blindness and, hence, castration.[11]

As in *Conducting Bodies,* the text of each of the three parts of *Triptych* consists of one single block of continuous prose. Within each section or panel of the triptych, the narrative thread passes back and forth from one story to another and from one particular scene of a story line to another, which raises the question of textual *framing.* This occurs when a scene which one supposes to be real is "captured" by a mimetic form, for example, the scene is transformed into a film, a poster, a book, and so on, which belongs to another one of the narrative sets. The effect is a retroactive subversion of the illusion of reality. Since *Triptych* is made up of a seemingly unending series of frames, nothing is "safe"; nothing is reserved or finally revealed as "real."[12]

In the following passage, the narrative thread passes from a scene belonging to story line B in the country to story line C in an industrial town in Flanders.

The aid of a knife has no doubt been necessary in order to dig into the layer upon layer of superimposed posters and enlarge the widest of the cracks made by the wood as it warped. The ocher circus ring has come unglued and rolled back on itself on one edge, baring the preceding poster. In the narrow triangle thus revealed, one can see a brick wall against which two silhouettes are locked in embrace. (6, 14)

And in the following passage, story line C is framed by story line A, the drama of the woman whose son is involved in drug-dealing.

[The man in the leather jacket] lifts the heavy machine up on the sidewalk, parks it on its stand, and then continues on foot. The interval between the two men diminishes from one lamppost to the next. Having arrived at this point in the story, which also marks the end of one chapter, the woman stops reading. (95, 126)

The book ends with a dual frame as the countryside of B is transformed into a jigsaw puzzle which is both completed and then broken up by Mr. Brown, the friend of Corinne. Finally, the focus shifts and this scene is transformed into the closing frames of a movie projected in the cinema on the street mentioned in the previous quotation.

[The river's] overflow runs down over a low wall, perpendicular to the middle piling of the bridge, forming a little cascade, the water then flowing rapidly again, glistening in the sun, between steep banks on which clumps of water willows and enormous bluish green leaves shaped like little ruffled collars or flaring funnels are growing. Leaning forward, his thighs parted, his left forearm resting on his left thigh, the man with the powerful but heavy build sets the last little piece in place with his right hand, and the last little island of black lacquer disappears [...]. [...] He sits there motionless for a few seconds, then suddenly his right hand violently sweeps back and forth across the surface of the table, breaking up the puzzle and scattering the little pieces all about. [...] The seat bottoms are now slapping against the seat backs all over the auditorium, in a deafening chorus, and the house lights go on. (169–71, 223–25)

The result is a paradox, a kind of enigma machine whose effect prevents any realistic reading of this novel. But this is not all, for the subversive effects of such textual framing can involve even another novel. For example, in *Triptych,* there are references to Corinne, Lambert, and the narrator in *Histoire.*[13] At the same time, the story of the somewhat less than heartbroken mother and her drug-dealing son turns out to be a movie shown in a barn in the country as well as a theater in an industrial town, not to mention the numerous scenes where "Corinne" is seen as an actress playing a role in a B-grade movie being made on the French Riviera. However, if this is the case, then not only *Histoire,* but also *all* of the other novels in the Reixach Cycle are potentially "framed" by *Triptych.* The reappearance of familiar characters now has become one of the principal techniques, not for the creation, but rather for the subversion or deconstruction of a whole fictive universe! The ultimate "lesson" is that the novel reveals itself as a product of human labor, a work of art that has its own rules and freedoms. A novel creates the illusion of reality, but it is no more the thing or the scene described than a picture postcard is the place portrayed. The ultimate paradox is that Simon's beautiful prose appears so realistic that readers are still apt to believe in this evocative illusion of reality, at least until they come upon the next textual frame.[14]

The novel includes a multitude of scenes, each of which eventually leads to the next, which cuts off the previous one. Thus, the points of juncture between scenes are of crucial importance, whether they be founded on a chromatic harmony, an erotic echo, a verbal allusion, or a thematic constant. In a novel in which so many textual intersections occur, it is not surprising that we should come across the old woman with the doglike face again and again. Among the places where Hecate was likely to appear were crossroads, and it was there that special food was left in her honor, in front of statues that represented her as a woman with *three* heads or bodies. Simon's *Triptych* is a fitting, and also a very modern, "sacrifice" to a goddess destined to appear to readers whose travels take them to these textual crossroads.

NOTES

1. "I had the project of writing a novel which would be irreducible to any realist schema, that is to say, a novel where the relationships among the different 'scenes' or 'sets' would in no way be constructed from any sequence or determinism of a psychological order, or from any similarity of situations or themes (like that of wandering without end which dominated *Conducting Bodies*), and where moreover there would be no privileged character, time or space" (Claude Si-

mon in *Claude Simon: analyse, théorie,* p. 424, quoted in English by David Carroll, *The Subject in Question,* p. 188).

2. *The Battle of Pharsalus,* 42–46; *La Bataille de Pharsale,* 65–71.

3. Cf. *Francis Bacon* (Exhibition at the Grand Palais, Paris, Oct. 26, 1971-Jan. 10, 1972). Other artists whose paintings influenced Simon in writing *Triptych* are Jean Dubuffet and Paul Delvaux (cf. Claud DuVerlie, "Interview with Claude Simon," *Sub- Stance* 8 [1974]: 4).

4. The cover of the French edition gives the following description of a triptych painting: "Although the actions or characters portrayed may have more or less close links (for example, several episodes of the same legend), other times the subjects of each of the panels are different. But, either way, the whole of the work constitutes an organic whole, both by the unity of its construction and the calculated manner in which the different forms and colors correspond with each other from one panel to another."

5. Cf. Simon's New York speech in *Three Decades of the French New Novel,* ed. Oppenheim, pp. 72–73.

6. See Georges Raillard's review of *Triptyque* in *Les Cahiers du Chemin* 18 (1973): 96–106.

7. *Triptych,* trans. Helen Lane (New York: Viking, 1976), p. 60; *Triptyque* (Paris: Minuit, 1973), p. 82. Subsequent references will appear in parentheses.

8. On the fascinating intertextual links that exist between Simon's first and eleventh novels, see A. C. Pugh, "Du *Tricheur* à *Triptyque,* et inversement," *Etudes littéraires* 9.1 (1976): 137–60.

9. Cf. "Armed once again with her knife, with only the point of the blade jutting out past her clenched fist, the old woman with the head like a dog's gouges out one of the rabbit's eyes with a brusque movement of her wrist" (18, 29–30).

10. The body of the dead rabbit and the penis are described in similar terms (cf. p. 113 and p. 143 in English, p. 86 and p. 188 in French).

11. "Now and then one catches a glimpse of the gleaming blade of a knife being held in the gnarled yellow fingers of her other hand. The girl lying in the hay accompanies with jerks of her hips the rhythmic back-and-forth motion of the buttocks of the man [. . .]" (15, 25); "With her rain-soaked hair dangling down like that of a drowned woman, her blind eyes of a drowned woman wide open in

the darkness, she appears to be unaware of the outside world, and the noise of the man's panting breath against her neck relegates to a vague background the various intermittent sounds that seem to be coming from very far away [. . .]" (39–40, 56). On castration in Simon, see Dällenbach, *Claude Simon,* pp. 86–88.

12. Cf. "All frames in the novel are relative and interested—no one frame, even that of the novel itself revealing or making visible its own visibility so that it will be perceived and privileged by the reader, is ever adequate, closed, or fixed" (Carroll, *The Subject in Question,* p. 195).

13. Cf. pp. 35–36, 76; pp. 51–52, 102.

14. See "La fin des illusions totalisantes *(Triptyque)*" in Dällenbach, *Le Récit spéculaire,* pp. 193–200.

CHAPTER NINE

The World About Us
(Leçon de choses)

The third in the trilogy of novels Simon wrote in the
70s, *Leçon de choses* (1975) is his shortest novel (only
176 pages in the original) published to date. Like *Triptych, The World About Us* offers a more finely tuned
version of *Conducting Bodies,* in that any reductive or
naïvely realistic reading of the text is made impossible
by the continual subversion of each of the various narrative sets by all the others. As in *Triptych,* Simon
chose to combine this technique of writing with some
of the subject matter that he had used in the novels of
his second period, the thematics of war borrowed from
The Flanders Road and *The Battle of Pharsalus.* The
1975 novel takes its title from the name of a textbook
used to teach French elementary school students about
practical things—both man-made objects and natural
phenomena—such as how houses are built or how cliffs
are formed.[1] Simon has an obvious nostalgia for the
lessons and the textbooks of bygone schooldays, although he always uses them in his own special way.
One thinks of the geometry problem in *Triptych,* the
Latin translation in *Histoire* and *The Battle of Pharsalus,* and the dictionary entries in *Conducting Bodies.*

The World About Us is Simon's answer to accusa-
tions made about modern experimental fiction that it

is "too dry," that it has "nothing to do with the real world," and that "it is too theoretical" and therefore "too far removed from readers' everyday concerns." In fact, Simon's French publisher included a *Prière d'insérer,* or insert, with the novel which must surely count as one of the most ironic publicity blurbs ever published.

> Aware of some of the faults that have been found with writers who neglect the "big problems," the author has attempted to tackle some of them here, such as the problems of habitat, manual labor, food, time, space, nature, leisure activities, education, discourse, information, adultery, destruction and reproduction of human and animal species. *It is a vast program which the millions of books which fill thousands of libraries are apparently far from having exhausted.*
>
> Although this little work [*travail*] does not claim to furnish the right solutions, its purpose is to contribute, in its own humble way and *within the limits of the genre,* to the general effort. [My trans.; emphasis added.]

What is surprising is that this hardly unambitious program is fulfilled, and that one way or another Simon's short novel does treat all the subjects mentioned in the description! One could even add to the list of subjects so that it would include class conflict, immigrant workers, child care, male chauvinism, and birth control. The operative words are "within the limits of the genre," the novel. The other important word used to describe the novel is "work," for the principal theme of the book is work, just as its own composition provides the reader with an excellent example of how the novelist works with and through words. From this point of view, another and equally valid title would be "Leçon de mots" (World of Words), for in the world of texts, there can be no things without words.

The novel opens as follows:

> The loose strips [*langues*] of wallpaper hang down to reveal damp, gray plaster, crumbling and flaking [*tombe*] onto the tiled floor before the brown baseboard [*plinthe*] whose upper edge is covered by a powdery film of whitish dust. Just above this edge [*plinthe*] runs a braid (or band?) in green-ocher and reddish (faded vermillion) shades with a repeated motif (frieze?) of acanthus leaves forming a succession of involuted waves.[2]

The description appears to be of a room in a house which is in a state of disrepair or perhaps being torn down. Despite the apparent exactness and detail of the description, the reader cannot help noting a certain hestitation in the choice of words: "a braid (or a band?)," "a repeated motif (frieze?)," as though the writer were not sure of certain technical words used to describe architectural details. More important, a word such as *bandeau,* "band," is part of a larger family of words in French that includes *bandage,* "bandage," *bande,* "group" (as in group of walkers), the verb *bander,* "to cover" (e.g. someone's eyes) *and* "to have an erection." By the not so innocent technique of hesitating over the choice of words, Simon's prose opens itself up to the seemingly infinite capacity of the writer to play with the meanings of words. Furthermore, many of the words used in this opening passage have double meanings in the original French. The strips of wallpaper hanging down are referred to as *langues* ("strips," but also "tongues," as well as "languages"); the falling plaster conjures up images of death (*tombe,* "falls," but also "tomb"); and the skirting board of the room (*plinthe*) could be read as its homonym, *plainte* ("complaint"). Finally, the frieze in the wall is like a "succession of *waves,*" which evokes both ocean waves and the waves of passion.

Readers familiar with the generative processes which Simon uses in his writing will not be surprised to learn that this novel is, among other things, about a complaining tongue, a fall, or rather several falls, and that one of the fictional series takes place near the sea. The room itself is alternately the scene of a military debacle, the place of work where two masons are tearing down a wall, and a construction site visited by some holidayers. This text will be built using the generative power of several of the words which the opening has already sown in the reader's mind. In Simon, construction of a new novel goes hand in hand with the subversion and deconstruction of older forms and discourses, such as that of his earlier war novels, not to mention this writer's traditional *bête noire,* the conventional novel that does not challenge any of the (lazy) reader's assumptions and preconceived ideas. Here, there is an implicit contrast between, on the one hand, the content of this opening sequence—a scene of destruction—and, on the other, the title of the section from which it is taken, "Generic," which refers to the opening credits in a movie. The words and the action of the novel that is being written or constructed are here being set in place. While things may wear out and end up in a state of decay, the words used to describe what is apparently the most neutral of scenes are always already heavy with implicit secondary meanings. Such is the way of *The World About Us* when reading Simon's rich prose.

As in *Triptych,* the author has included three narrative sets whose story lines are entwined throughout the novel. Furthermore, each of the story lines can be associated with one of the following themes: war, work, and love.

A. Three French soldiers—a gunner, a loader and an ammunition-server—attempt to defend an old house about to be attacked by the Germans during World War II. While waiting, one of the soldiers reads an old textbook entitled *The World About Us.*

B. Two masons—one of whom was an artilleryman during the war—demolish a wall in an old house. During the lunch break, the former soldier tells his younger colleague about his experiences during the war.

C. A group of holidayers walk along a cliff at the seaside. Their clothes and behavior would appear to belong to the nineteenth century. Indeed, they are frozen in time as if they had been plucked out of a painting by Claude Monet (1840–1926) or Eugène Boudin (1824–98).[3] Two of the holidayers, a man and a woman, meet at night for a prearranged rendezvous and make love while an audience of cows looks on. The group of walkers end up by visiting a house under construction, perhaps the same one in the other two fictional series, in which they see a sign warning about the danger of a short-circuit.

As a critic has pointed out, all three of the narrative series revolve around the notion of death: the soldiers are dying of fear as well as wounds, the workers are dead tired, and the lovers meet for that "little death" (orgasm) described so frequently in Simon's novels.[4] The idea of a fall also serves to unify the various scenes from the different story lines. The wall that the workers are demolishing is falling down; the soldiers are holed up in an old house which, from the military point of view, is about to fall; and the scene of the vacationers walking along a cliff leads to what might be called rather tritely the "fall" of a married woman. In the newspaper headlines "quoted" toward the end of the text, the workers perish in the collapse of a building, the soldiers are killed, and the vacationers perish when the cliff they are walking along falls down.

The fact that *The World About Us* is composed of seven parts gives the novel a mathematical symmetry since the first and last, the second and sixth, the third and fifth chapters, respectively, correspond to each other in both structure and length.[5] The description of the room in "Generic" appears to be complete or exhaustive until we come upon the following sentence:

This description (construction) may be continued (or completed) more or less indefinitely depending on the exhaustiveness of the treatment, the elaboration of further metaphors, the addition of other objects, whether seen in their entirety or fragmented by wear, time, a blow (or whether only partly visible within the framework of the picture), not counting the various hypotheses to which the spectacle might lend support. (4, 10–11)[6]

Description as a generator of narrative continues to preoccupy Simon, and in fact one of the principal differences between *Triptych* and *The World About Us* is the greater attention paid in the later novel, not just to visual phenomena, which continue to predominate, but also to auditive, olfactive, tactile, and gustatory sensations. The second chapter, entitled "Expansion," introduces all the fictional sets of the novel. The third chapter, "Divertissement I," refers to a short ballet or musical piece played between longer pieces. As well, the word carries with it an echo of the famous pronouncement by Blaise Pascal (1623–62) about distractions which lead us imperceptibly to our death.[7] In this section, descriptive prose gives way to a monologue spoken by one of the World War II soldiers in a colloquial style replete with sexual innuendo. The central section of the book bears the same title as the novel itself. Like a perfect scale model, the title thus refers both to the book read by one of the soldiers under attack and to the novel in which it is embedded. In the fifth chapter, "Divertissement II," the complaining voice is that of the older mason who is probably the same as that of the soldier who foretold imminent doom and defeat in "Divertissement I." "The Reichshoffen Charge" refers to a French cavalry charge during the Franco-Prussian War.[8] It is redolent with the nineteenth century, but also with death and defeat, all of which apply to the nighttime rendezvous of the adulterous couple. The sexual scenes in *The World About Us,* which allude to Flaubert's *Madame Bovary* (1857), are Simon's most vivid evocation of male chauvinism and the sexual abuse of women. Finally, in "Short Circuits" all the narrative threads of the novel cross, intersect, and subvert each other.

Despite the fact that the entire novel is told in the

present tense, there are at least three different and distinctive uses of language in *The World About Us:* the authoritative and apparently naïve prose of the textbook; the slangy run-on monologues of the soldier and the mason; and finally the luxuriant style of the rest of the novel. One could label the three styles respectively as prosaic, colloquial, and descriptive; however, a careful reading of the novel reveals just how interrelated they are. Compared to *Triptych,* the monologues of *The World About Us* are the principal stylistic innovation of a novel in which sounds play such an important part, for the musicality of Simon's prose can be appreciated throughout the entire novel.[9]

Once again a novel by Simon is its own best (self-) commentary as language demonstrates itself to be infinitely polysemic. Metaphors abound and many of them are self-reflexive since they are to be found in descriptions contained in a text(book) of the same name as the book we are reading. Despite the differences in style, the two books are not all that different in point of fact. Whether it be for the construction of walls or novels, mortar of one kind or another is essential in joining together the various building blocks involved in two types of work illustrated by this novel, that is, masonry and writing. This is just one example, but the reader familiar with Simon will have no trouble discerning to what extent the novel may be read as a scale model of itself. Furthermore, since it thematicizes so successfully a paradox inherent in all of Simon's writing—the conflicting tendencies to order and disorder, to structure and disintegration, to construction and deconstruction—*The World About Us* could well be considered as a scale model of all Simon's work(s).

NOTES

1. "The object lesson evokes elementary school and the calm authority of a Third Republic-type teacher whose task it is to instill [in his students] a sense of objective and methodic observation of things as the first step in the formation of a scientific mind" (Colette Gaudin, "Niveaux de lisibilité dans *Leçon de choses* de Claude Simon," *Romanic Review* 68.3 [1977]: 179 [my trans.]).

2. *The World About Us,* trans. Daniel Weissbort (Princeton, NJ: Ontario Review Press, 1983), pp. 3 and 119; *Leçon de choses* (Paris: Minuit, 1975), pp. 9 and 177. Subsequent references appear in the text.

3. See Michael Evans, "Two Uses of Intertextuality. References to Impressionist Painting and *Madame Bovary* in Claude Simon's *Leçon de choses*," *Nottingham French Studies* 19.1 (1980): 33–45.

4. Sykes, *Les Romans de Claude Simon,* p. 177.

5. "The narrative cunningly orchestrates disparate impressions into the verbal equivalent of a musical piece, inscribing the different incidents and leitmotivs into a fugal arrangement" (Mark Andrews, Introduction to *The World About Us,* p. ix).

6. For a detailed reading of "Generic," see Dällenbach, *Claude Simon,* pp. 104–26.

7. "[L]e divertissement nous amuse, et nous fait arriver insensiblement à la mort." (Pascal, *Pensées,* 2.171).

8. The charge ended in the annihilation of a division of armored cavalry on August 6, 1870.

9. See Roger Dragonetti, "Leçon de choses et Le son de choses," *MLN* 103.4 (1988): 751–68.

CHAPTER TEN

The Georgics
(*Les Géorgiques*)

Characters—some of whom are larger than life, some of whom the reader of Simon has already met—a family secret, a cache of old documents discovered 150 years after they were hidden, political intrigue, the end of an era, a debate about the decision to execute a king, two revolutions that lead to a reign of terror, Flanders, Naples, Tunis, Barcelona, the south of France, Paris, and even England—such is just some of the subject matter of *Les Géorgiques* (1981), Simon's longest and most significant novel published to date. Although there are similarities between this extremely dense text and those of the second and third manners, in fact, *The Georgics* represents a new style in and of itself, for Simon managed to combine and go beyond the various techniques of fiction-writing of his earlier works. On the one hand, the novel (re)tells the family romance familiar to readers of *Histoire,* while on the other, it weaves together three different stories, each of which colors our reading of the others, as in the more impersonal novels, *Triptych* and *The World About Us*. And like *The Palace* and *The Battle of Pharsalus, The Georgics* is largely, although by no means exclusively, devoted to the thematics of war.

The first fictional thread of the 1981 novel involves the personal life and public career of a character born in the middle of the eighteenth century—identified in the novel only by his initials, L. S. M.—who is in turn a soldier, officer, politician, and ambassador during three successive political regimes in France: the monarchy, the First Republic (1792–1804), and the First Empire (1804–1815), founded by Napoleon Bonaparte. The second fictional thread concerns a soldier in World War II who will remind readers of Georges in *The Flanders Road,* while the third recalls *The Palace* and *Histoire,* being about a foreigner who is in and around Barcelona during the Spanish Civil War. For readers who like to locate historical sources, the eighteenth-century soldier in *The Georgics* is modeled on a historical figure, Jean-Pierre Lacombe-Saint-Michel (1751–1812), one of Simon's ancestors.[1] What happens to the cavalry soldier in World War II is probably based on Simon's own wartime experience. Identified only as O., the Englishman caught up in the fighting and politics of wartorn Spain in the 1930s bears a strong resemblance to George Orwell (1903–50), the famous essayist and novelist who wrote *Animal Farm* (1946), *1984* (1949), and the book that Simon made use of in writing *The Georgics, Homage to Catalonia* (1938). In this case, the French novelist "re-writes" Orwell's narrative in his own inimitable style without quoting the original text, whereas in the case of the L. S. M. thread, Simon quotes from a wide variety of documents dealing with the personal lives of the characters and the political and military history of the period.

As is clear from even this very brief description of the novel, *The Georgics* is a complex narrative, moreover, one upon which Simon labored for many years, since an early version of the L. S. M. theme can be found in a short text published eight years before the novel finally saw the light of day.[2] Work is the principal theme of the novel. The importance attached to work (as a kind of supertheme that subsumes the other themes and leitmotifs) recalls *The World About Us,* the short novel Simon wrote while he was in the process of writing the much longer project represented by *The Georgics.* Simon himself is not ashamed—on the contrary—to speak of the hard work involved in writing a novel, for he sees himself as a workman and a maker of things,[3] etymologically a "poet," one who takes legitimate pride in his craft and the final product, a text, which when finished must stand on its own, as distinct from its creator as it is from any models he may have used. In *The Georgics,* Batti (L. S. M.'s faithful helper), the soldier, and the would-be revolutionary always have new fields to conquer, to work upon. It is certainly not by chance that in Simon's novel so much of this work involves the *written word:* from all parts of Europe L. S. M. writes to Batti giving her instructions about how to run the family estate in the south of France—what crops to sow, what animals to breed—so that in many ways her work is harder, although less heroic, according to the traditional scheme of things, than the General's more public accomplishments. At the same time, L. S. M. sends written orders to his subordinates and writes down his opinions concerning important political issues of the day when he is a member of the revolutionary government. Furthermore, there are many references to O.'s writing an account of his experiences in Spain during the civil war after

170

his return to England. Also, extracts are quoted from the letters of L. S. M.'s widow seeking redress from Louis XVIII for past injustices, not to mention the mysterious documents that were kept hidden by L. S. M.'s descendants.

Simon's 1981 novel is a composite of many elements, both thematic and narrative, and among those components there is also a strong element of suspense and mystery that revolves around the eighteenth-century narrative thread. However, despite the extensive use of history in *The Georgics,* it is not an ordinary historical novel. Rather, Simon's novel is based upon the textual dynamics, including the technique of intertextual cross-referencing, which readers of the author's earlier works will have come to know and appreciate. Apart from *The Battle of Pharsalus,* no other novel by Simon makes such effective use of the technique of intertextuality.[4] *The Georgics* is an integral part of Simon's *oeuvre,* and the links that bind it to the earlier texts are as solid as the internal links that bind the various constituent parts together. Like a detective looking for clues, the reader of Simon must constantly be on the alert for this is a demanding text and it requires active participation. Moreover, such a fundamentally *analogical* construction is also one of the best mystery stories ever written.

Simon has unabashedly recycled the title of a long didactic poem about agriculture written by the Latin poet Vergil (70–19 B.C.), entitled *Georgics* (29 B.C.). In the context of Simon's own *oeuvre,* the title makes one think of *Georges* Thomas in *The Grass* and *The Flanders Road,* since much of *The Georgics* recalls Georges's wartime experiences. Furthermore, one of the charac-

171

ters of the 1981 novel is presented as the author of an earlier novel about World War II. *The Georgics* could be considered as Georges's tale or epic. As well, the wrinkled skin of the soldier-cum-writer is compared to "crêpe *georgette*" ([17], 24), a kind of cloth used to make mourning clothes, recalling the many deaths in the family portrayed in *The Georgics* as well as *Histoire*. Within *The Georgics*, L. S. M. mentions in an account of his captivity in North Africa that the prime minister of Tunis is a *Georgian*. Finally, during the civil war in Spain, the Russian politico who takes over the day-to-day running of the government in Barcelona and is no doubt responsible for the outright physical elimination of any noncommunist leftists such as O., modeled after *George* Orwell, is known under several different pseudonyms, among which are *Grigoriev, Grigoriévitch, Goriev*. Thus, in its very title, *The Georgics* manages to combine the three fictional threads which it incorporates, the thread of the twentieth-century (ex-)soldier which goes back to *The Flanders Road* and *The Grass* where Georges Thomas appears as a would-be farmer, the thread of the Spanish Civil War which goes back to *The Palace* and *Histoire*, and finally, the thread of the eighteenth-century officer who is the ancestor of Charles and his nephew. Of course, it is the ancestor who is one of the most signficant sources for the title since so many of L. S. M.'s letters giving directives to Batti read like a textbook about agriculture.

To appreciate Simon's title fully, one must understand the etymology of the original Latin title of Vergil's poem, *Georgicon*, which is derived from the Greek *geôrgikos*. This word is itself composed of two elements, *gê* "earth" and *ergon* "work." Thus the title refers to the work of the fields. In Simon's novel the fields in question are not only the fields of L. S. M.'s family estate, but also the battlefields of revolutionary and postrevolutionary Europe over which L. S. M. labored for so many years at the end of the eighteenth and the beginning of the nineteenth centuries, as well as the (battle)fields of Catalonia and Flanders. Perhaps of greatest importance is the pure mass of pages that constitute the novel, the many pages which Simon has labored over. Labor here has only positive connotations, all the more so since in French, *labourer* means "to plow," for each line, like the furrows in a field, has been worked upon. *The Georgics* is, among other things, an eminently self-reflexive title since it refers to itself, to the labor that it cost Simon to write the novel. Finally, it would not be fair to neglect the readers' work, for they too must exert themselves in order to appropriate this narrative mosaic.

After an epigraph taken from the *Confessions* of Jean-Jacques Rousseau (1712–78),[5] the novel commences with an untitled prologue or preamble that begins:

> The scene is as follows: in a room of vast dimensions a character is seated at a desk, with one of his legs half tucked under his chair, the heel of the foot raised, with his right foot forward flat on the ground, the tibia forming with the thigh an angle of about forty-five degrees, with his two arms leaning on the edge of the desk, his hands holding up in front of him a piece of paper (a letter?) which he is staring at. The character is naked. ([7], 11)[6]

Recalling the opening of *Triptych,* we know from the outset that we are reading about a scene. At first we do not know what kind of scene, for it could be a theatrical tableau, a painting, or, as it turns out, a drawing. Nothing in the opening lines informs us about the identity of the persons represented in the drawing whose style recalls the magnificent sketches of the eighteenth-century artist and revolutionary Jacques Louis David (1748–1825) for his painting, *Oath of the Jeu de Paume.* Nor do we immediately know when or where the scene takes place. The key elements are the vast space of the room, the character seated at a desk, the almost clinical details about the position of his body, and the action he is performing, that is, apparently reading or just staring at a document which may be a letter. (This scene of reading reprises the beginning of *The Flanders Road* in which de Reixach reads a letter sent to him by Georges's mother.) The nakedness of the human body described seems to indicate a kind of zero degree of character. However, even the nakedness of the character is made problematical for he is in fact not entirely naked. In the drawing, parts of a military uniform have been added, complete with colors. Thus the character described has an ambiguous status: both clothed and unclothed, both Everyman and a particular character in a specific historical situation and context, while the scene of which he is a part is curiously represented as at once finished and incomplete. It is not hard to realize that the figure described represents the archetypal Simonian character at this stage in the development of the novelist's career. On the one hand, he has rejected the personalized characters of conventional fiction. On the other, there is still an element of (hi)story left to explore, describe, and color in. Simon is telling us here that the novel we are reading is neither part of the earlier Reixach Cycle nor the later and more impersonal trilogy of the 1970s. Rather we are dealing with a truly "new novel," one in which Simon is setting out to explore new avenues in fiction-writing.[7]

Later in the prologue Simon writes as follows: "It is obvious that the interpretation of such a drawing is possible only according to a code of writing which both parties, the draftsman and the viewer, have agreed upon in advance" ([8], 13). Of course, what is valid for the artist and the viewer is also valid for the writer and the reader. What new readers of Simon should realize is that, however difficult his novels at first may appear, they also teach us how to read them. The code referred to above is not a secret message to which only certain privileged readers have access, but rather the willingness of writer and reader alike to acknowledge that portions of the finished work of art may represent scenes which are more complete than others, while some may only be sketched in, to use an artistic image. Such a "code of writing" implies just that, that we are dealing with a cultural object and that for it to function properly, writer and reader must agree on certain implicit rules of the game. What is interesting in this case is that the code which the prologue sets in place is one in which the realistic conventions of traditional representation (whether in the visual arts or narrative texts) have been deliberately infringed upon, exposed, and subverted for all to see and read.

The Georgics consists of six parts: a prologue not named as such and five numbered parts. As mentioned, the prologue describes a drawing in which an almost naked officer is portrayed reading a document of some kind. Later on, we learn of the existence of another younger character who remains standing in a rather arrogant manner before his superior. The two characters in this initial scene may be interpreted as L. S. M. and a fellow officer, perhaps one bringing him news of the family, or alternatively as the older Simon confronting his younger self or Orwell, or perhaps even as Simon and his reader.

Part 1 is devoted to all three of the fictional series: L. S. M., Charles's nephew and O.[8] This part is in turn divided by asterisks into three sections, each of which is characterized by a distinctive use of typographic characters. In pages 15–25, roman characters are used to describe the adventures of L. S. M., while italics are used to describe scenes which center on the stories of the twentieth-century soldier/writer and O. In the second section (25–36), the typographical system is reversed, since italics are used to describe the adventures of L. S. M. while roman characters are utilized for the stories of O., the boy and the soldier (the latter two being younger "incarnations" of the man who later writes a novel about his wartime experiences). Finally, in the last section, (36–51), no italics are used and the third-person pronoun "he" refers to all three of the characters. Given that so much of the fiction depends upon the similarity of the experiences of these different characters, it is fitting that no further distinction be made at this point in our reading of the novel.

Part 2 is entirely devoted to the experiences of Charles's nephew as a cavalryman in World War II during the winter and spring of 1939–40.

Part 3, the longest chapter in the book, is about the former cavalryman's visit to the estate of L. S. M. in order to see the grave of his ancestor's first wife. The visit described forms a long narrative parenthesis within the larger context of the story of the boy's growing up with his grandmother and Uncle Charles in the old family home which readers of Simon will recognize from *Histoire*.

In part 4 the fictional locus shifts to Spain, for this section centers on the adventures of O. in Barcelona (as well as the Aragon front) during the period 1936–37. The narrator also describes O.'s attempts to write down, after his return to England, the traumatic experiences through which he just lived. Just as part 2 can be seen to consitute a kind of addition to *The Flanders Road* and part 3 as a further development of *Histoire,* so too part 4 can be considered as a return to some of the themes of *The Palace*.

Part 5 is devoted to L. S. M.: events concerning his personal life and military career as well as others that happened after the death of the old soldier. The invisible third-person narrator of the novel relies both on documents and his own imagination as he tells the story to which Charles alludes at the end of part 3 and which has been lost sight of for so long, the many years that L. S. M.'s descendants kept it hidden *and* the time that it has taken us to read part 4! In doing so, the narrator creates a magnificent (inter)textual collage of document and narrative, of quotation and description. By now, this tale of war, revolution, and family conflict has acquired so much textual resonance, so many structural echoes and mnemonic harmonics, that one reads it literally in depth, that is, through the other parts of the novel.

As in the novels of the Reixach Cycle, *The Georgics* will be understood better if readers can visualize the family relationships of the characters involved (except for O., who remains an outsider). Given the close links between *The Georgics* and *Histoire,* I have included characters from both novels. Names of characters from *Histoire* are in regular print; those from *The Georgics* are in *italics;* and those from both *Histoire* and *The Georgics* are in CAPITALS. Names of characters only alluded to in *The Georgics* are in square brackets.

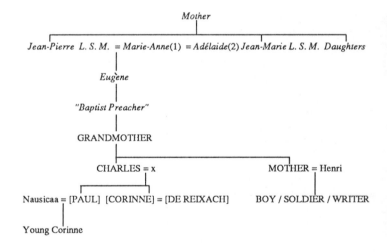

Readers of the earlier novels will remember that de Reixach and the World War II soldier were central characters in *The Flanders Road;* that Corinne appeared in *The Flanders Road, The Battle of Pharsalus,* and *Triptych;* the grandmother, Uncle Charles and the soldier in *The Battle of Pharsalus*. One can conceive of the family tree as a group of branches which has grown in a nonchronological, nonlinear way. De Reixach and Corinne are like generators of a series of ever-expanding sets of characters. Their relationship, which is at the center of *The Flanders Road,* is further explored in *Histoire,* which fleshes out Corinne's family background (her parents, her brother Paul and his continuation of the family line, her cousin [first seen in *The Palace*], his mother and father, the grandmother). *The Battle of Pharsalus* does not add new characters to the familial drama. However, *Triptych* does sketch in Corinne's son while at the same time undermining his mother as a "real" character since she turns out to be the role of an actress in a B-grade movie.[9] Now comes *The Georgics* which explores the grandmother's ancestors, thereby subsuming or containing the earlier novels. Given the central position of de Reixach (related to Sabine in *The Grass* and *The Flanders Road* as well as the eighteenth-century Reixach of *The Flanders Road* and *Histoire*), it becomes obvious just how much of Simon's fiction can be considered to form an organic whole. Even *The World About Us* could be included since (de) Reixach is named in the soldier's diatribe against war,[10] leaving only *Conducting Bodies* outside this series of interrelated sagas, although one could possibly identify the Soldier/Writer of *The Georgics* with the participant at the writers' conference in South America in the earlier novel.

It is possible to identify Charles's nephew, the adolescent who goes to the cinema on Sunday afternoons, as the same character as the cavalryman of World War II, and the writer of a book about his wartime experiences. Furthermore, the wrinkled hands of the anonymous reader leafing through L. S. M.'s papers would appear to be another incarnation of the same character. The soldier's boyhood experiences closely parallel those of the narrator of *Histoire* and like Georges in *The Flanders Road* and the soldier character in *The Battle of Pharsalus,* the twentieth-century soldier in *The Georgics* is a cavalryman in the French army during the early part of World War II. From a realistic point of view, it is obvious that Charles's nephew (*Histoire*) and Louise's husband (*The Grass, The Flanders Road*) are not the same character. Nonetheless, in terms of the textual and organic unity of Simon's *oeuvre,* it is possible to include all the various manifestations of the Farmer/Soldier/Writer under one fictional rubric, a kind of proto-Georges who gives his name to the title of the 1981 novel. As to the narrator of the novel itself, he is a third-person narrator about whom nothing is said. From the discursive position he occupies it is possible to deduce that he may be still another incarnation of the Boy/Soldier/Writer.[11]

O., an English journalist and idealist, travels to Spain to write about the civil war, but he ends up joining a faction of the prorevolutionary forces whose members are later hunted down, arrested, and summarily executed by rival groups that are supposedly on the same side. As in *The Palace,* the politics of Spain

in 1936–37 are shown to be far less clearcut than some
of the rather naïve volunteers in the International Brigade had thought at first. As such, O.'s role is that of
a kind of strawman whose political naïveté makes him
an easy target of the narrator's irony. While some of
the experiences of O. recall those of the ex-student in
The Palace and *Histoire,* who was no less naïve than
the Englishman at the time, the chief difference is the
way the two former volunteers wrote about their experiences in Barcelona. Whereas the ex-student turned
his memories into pages of descriptive prose that evoke
the political confusion, the fear and apprehension, indeed the outright panic experienced at the time *in and
through the writing,* O. is portrayed in *The Georgics*
as attempting to write an account based on the twin
resources of grammar and chronology.

> Perhaps he hopes that by writing down his adven-
> ture he will be able to make some kind of coherent
> sense out of it. From the outset the fact that he is
> going to enumerate in their chronological order
> events which are rushing about at random in his
> memory or which present themselves according to
> affective priorities should, to a certain extent, ex-
> plain them. He also thinks perhaps that within this
> first order the obligations of syntax will make cause
> and effect relations stand out. However, there will
> be holes in his story, obscure points, even things that
> are incoherent. [. . .] In fact, as he writes his feelings
> of helplessness and utter confusion do not cease to
> grow. ([209–10], 310–11)

Once again, Simon's point is that history cannot be
told in a logical or rational manner if the account is
be truly meaningful for the reader. Hence the section

of *The Georgics* devoted to the trials and tribulations of O. before and after his return to England takes the form of a rewriting in Simon's inimitable style of parts of *Homage to Catalonia*. It is as though Simon were giving a lesson to Orwell on how he might have written about the war in Spain.

One of the most important elements missing in the Englishman's narrative of his adventures in Spain is textual depth, whereas in Simon's novel, the experiences of O. form only a part of a long and complex text. As provocative as Simon's retelling of that tale may be, it only takes on real significance within the context of *The Georgics* when read alongside and even through the adventures of the other characters in the novel, for the emphasis in Simon is squarely on the recurrence of similar events over the centuries. For example, the nasty turn that the Spanish revolution takes in 1937 recalls the Terror of the French Revolution in 1792–94. Furthermore, in Simon's novel Barcelona acquires an indepth resonance when it is read not only as the site of O.'s mishaps but also as the last career posting of L. S. M. This raises the larger question of the intertextual (as opposed to causal) relations that can be discerned among Simon's own novels, not to mention those that unite them to other texts such as Orwell's. Played before the reader's eyes, *The Georgics* effectively creates a drama that subsumes the stories of the individual actors so that in the end all the various narrative threads are woven together in one vast textual fabric.

Charles, the Boy/Soldier's uncle, is essentially the same character whom the reader met in *Histoire* and *The Battle of Pharsalus*. As in the two earlier novels, he is occupied with wine-making and talking about the lives and experiences of others. Closeted in the confines of his dark study with its drawn shutters, Charles lives vicariously. In *The Georgics* he is responsible for transmitting the L. S. M. papers to his nephew, documents which he describes as "at once fastidious and fascinating." He acts as the link, the messenger, between, on the one hand, the dying—and later on dead—world of the grandmother (his mother) anchored in the bourgeois values of the late nineteenth century and, on the other hand, the modern world of the twentieth century to which the former soldier belongs. Unlike his mother, Charles refuses to hide the family skeletons in the proverbial closet where they lay for so long, and unlike the narrator, Charles himself is incapable of doing anything with them except to talk about them in a vague sort of way.

While her daughter, Charles's sister, remains unseen, literally offstage where she is presumably occupied with her illness and approaching death (cf. *Histoire*), the grandmother takes charge of the household. Like Batti in the eighteenth century, she is a true matriarch. Concerned with keeping up social appearances, the grandmother insists on the elaborate rituals of formal entertaining despite the family's relative poverty: even on her deathbed, she is worried lest there be not enough wine to drink at her wake! The last living descendant of L. S. M. to bear his name, she is responsible for hiding much of the truth about her family's past. For years she zealously guards a roll of old wallpaper which she uses to repaper the stairwell in order to hide the door to the closet where the papers of her famous ancestor lie hidden until after her death.

In many ways, the grandmother represents the nine-teenth-century reaction to the French Revolution, since she explicitly reproaches her ancestor with voting for the death of Louis XVI. According to her version of history, the Convention decided to execute the king by a majority of one:

> [. . .] as if a single one of the three hundred and sixty-one sacrilegious votes condensed in him the filth of the blood shed, as if the death of the king-martyr had only been due to a single wish, that of a single murderer who not only bore her name but had fathered the father of her father [. . .]. ([103], 150)

Paradoxically, this great-grandchild of a revolutionary is herself a reactionary who idealizes the past and the old ways of pre-Revolutionary France. The scenes where the narrator describes clandestine visits to the cinema form a vivid contrast with the very different social rite to which the grandmother initiated her grandson by taking him to a performance of the opera *Orfeo ed Euridice* (1762) by Christoph von Gluck (1714–87).[12] To the boy's own surprise, it is at the opera that he experiences a greater sense of transgression.

The most attractive female character in *The Georgics* is Batti. It is Batti who grew up in the L. S. M. household, who welcomes Jean-Pierre's Dutch wife, Marie-Anne, to her position as first lady of the chateau, who takes care of her new mistress until the latter's death, who labors long and hard to read the detailed instructions which Jean-Pierre sends her from all corners of France and Europe on how to run the farm, who attempts to carry out his directives, and who ends up receiving nothing but a severe reprimand about how she has failed her master by not providing him with enough wine and linen! After L. S. M.'s death, Batti is accused by his second wife, Adélaïde, of helping her former master's son rob the widow of her rightful inheritance. Closer to the earth and the animals she takes care of than to most human beings, Batti represents a kind of earth mother condemned to sterility, not unlike Marie in *The Grass,* because of her unrequited love for L. S. M., who played erotic games with her in their adolescence.

Described as a giant of a man, Jean-Pierre L. S. M. is the maternal great-great-great-grandfather of the boy who later participates in and writes about World War II.[13] L. S. M.'s life reads like a novel, to coin an expression, although Simon's deliberate juxtaposition of different periods as well as the use of the Republican calendar (1792 = Year I) tend to blur the chronology. A boy soldier in the king's army, the adult L. S. M. refuses to fire on the citizens of Paris during the taking of the Bastille in 1789. He participates in the Revolution and is elected to the legislative body known as the Convention, where he votes for the death of Louis XVI in 1793. He then takes part in the subsequent European wars as France seeks to defend and export her revolution. In 1799 at the time of Nelson's love affair with Lady Hamilton, L. S. M. finds himself in Naples which he is forced to leave in a small boat because of the Neopolitan court's hostility to regicides (Caroline, the Queen of Naples, was Marie Antoinette's sister). During his escape, he is captured by Barbary pirates and held prisoner in North Africa where he is befriended by the Bey, or governor, of Tunis, and while there he buys a stallion which he names Mustapha after one of the Bey's relatives. After returning to France, he escapes the Terror with his life intact and with a new (royalist!) wife in tow. At one point his brilliant career seems to slow down mysteriously as he is given lackluster postings. L. S. M. ends his career as military governor of Barcelona, a tired and sick though not very old man. He returns to his estate in the south of France to spend one last year, that cycle of the four seasons, on his own land, in the company not of his second wife and son, but rather of his memories and his old and faithful servant, Batti. Walled up in the huge house as though in some giant tomb, L. S. M. seems to have taken to the grave a secret too terrible to tell.

> For there was something hidden there. Something had closed over it [the chateau] that had struck it like lightning and yet kept it standing, like a tomb, a mutilated watchman, for which it was called upon to bear witness and to pay: not the simple crime of beheading of a monarch [...] but something (what can one call it: the event, the tragedy, the secret?: no one ever spoke of it in the family) that had shaken it up (the family) right to its very entrails and after which it too (the chateau) had been condemned, abandoned to its death [...]. ([103–04], 150)

Jean-Pierre belonged to a generation of men who believed in Progress and who thought that they could construct a new and supposedly better world order, one without kings and class privilege. However, given the strange course of history, L. S. M. ends up working for an emperor, Napoleon Bonaparte, and his royalist widow will live on to see the restoration of the monarchy. Although L. S. M.'s numerous exploits seem to make him an important historic figure, after his death little if anything will remain of his life and works. By the time the former soldier of 1940 undertakes his research into his ancestor's life, the family farm and home in which L. S. M. took so much interest are in a state of almost total ruin. Even L. S. M.'s grave has been destroyed by excavations for a highway. It is as though fate had deliberately set out to undo as many of the soldier's achievements as possible: even the marble bust of the late great warrior disappears, sold off by one of his descendants. As for the name, the Soldier/Writer's grandmother was the last to bear it, and she did so with a kind of haughty shame. All that remains then is the paper covered by the handwriting of L. S. M. and his various secretaries. This mass of writing would seem to constitute an odd kind of monument to such a man of action until one realizes that for L. S. M., as well as for the present-day Soldier-cum-Writer, action and language, writing and making things happen, are intimately tied up.

But this is not all, and in fact if *The Georgics* were limited to the characters already mentioned, it would not be the aesthetic success that it is. Although alert readers may discern an early clue which Simon has taken care to plant,[14] it is not until the end of part 3 that we definitely learn of the solution to the mystery that lies at the center of the novel:

> [. . .] Uncle Charles stuffing the tobacco into the bowl of his pipe, lighting it, drawing several puffs, then raising his eyes: "Because he had a brother . . . ," and

the boy: "A br . . . What brother?," and Uncle Charles:
"Legally and biologically. Yes. Because it is custom-
ary to give that name to the products of two embryos
produced by the same male glands and nurtured in
the same womb. Except that they resembled each
other about as much as a negative resembles a photograph. Which is to say exactly the same and exactly opposite . . . ," and the boy: "Then he had a
brother? But why . . . ," and Uncle Charles: "You
mean: why didn't anyone ever speak about him?
There you have it: precisely!" ([171–72], 255–56)

So it turns out that the terrible secret, which the old
soldier kept walled up inside himself and which the
grandmother was able to hide until long after her own
death almost 150 years after the fact, concerns nothing
less than the life and death of a younger L. S. M.
brother who was executed by firing squad for betraying
the Revolution in which Jean-Pierre played such an
active part! Jean-Marie comes by his name well, for
there is a fundamental femaleness about him. Firstly,
he rebels against the phallocentric ethic of war and
revolution (made by and for middle-class French men)
espoused by his brother. Secondly, Jean-Marie, like
Batti, leaves no text, no written trace behind him. The
only documents that remain, including the military
tribunal's decision to have him executed, are written
by others. Like *The Grass, The Georgics* is also, at least
in part, a poignant memorial to the female—unwritten
and hidden—side of history since it incorporates and
writes the story of what traditional historians would
consider to be two nonentities, two of history's all-time
losers: Batti, the unsung heroine of the home front, and
Jean-Marie, a renegade who chose the "wrong" side.

Unlike his brother, Jean-Marie rebels against the military hierarchy and the revolutionary ethic of his time. His rejection of war and killing reminds one of the World War II cavalryman and O., at least to the extent that they too demonstrate great cynicism about the value of such "heroic" enterprises as killing fellow human beings and creating new world orders. For today's reader, Jean-Marie is the brother who appears the more interesting and sensitive of the two L. S. M.'s, for it is he, and not the one-time hero, who is the literary ancestor of today's outsiders. It is not by chance, that some of the most moving and best-written passages of *The Georgics* treat the L. S. M. brother who had no children and therefore no descendants, who rebelled against war and revolution, and who was shot in the name of so-called Liberty, Equality, and Fraternity:

[. . .] that outlaw who roamed in the woods like a poacher, who didn't even own a horse, and of whom not a trace, not a locket, not a letter, not a single piece of paper would later remain to bear witness to his existence (except those two simple words: my brother, when it came time to divide up his belongings, and that poster [announcing his trial and judgment] [. . .]). ([285], 420)

In a novel filled with textual echoes, the theme of brotherhood provides the narrative with an overall unity that extends across the various time frames and geographical loci of the stories told. There are at least six brotherlike relationships just as there are six parts in the novel. Jean-Pierre and O. both live through revolutions which turn to institutionalized violence.

Jean-Marie and the twentieth-century soldier form another pair of brothers. Related by blood, they are both disillusioned with war, and as such both of them could be considered as foils to Jean-Pierre, the career soldier. As for Jean-Marie and O., the two renegades, both of them live on the run, hunted down like wild animals by terrorists who have assumed total political control of a country or a city. The Boy/Soldier-cum-Writer and O. form another pair of brothers-in-arms. Though unrelated by blood, these citizens of the twentieth century are witnesses to two of the bloodiest adventures of our times. If one identifies the Boy/Soldier with the narrator of *The Georgics,* one can even discern a strong case of sibling rivalry! The many documents Jean-Pierre left behind him are part of the Boy/Soldier's ancestral heritage, part of his family's illustrious and infamous roots. Although the eighteenth- and the twentieth-century soldiers do not appear to be of similar character, the differences between these two brothers are erased by the parallel circumstances in which they find themselves in both war and peace. When the Boy/Soldier, who himself has become an old man by then, leafs through his ancestor's papers, the narrative focuses, as in a cinematographic close-up, on the wrinkled skin of his hands (cf. part 1). But they could also be the hands of L. S. M. at the end of his life as he casts a nostalgic glance at the memorabilia he has accumulated throughout the years of his military career. Just as the long-since dried ink has formed a fine mica-like powder, so too both men, both *bodies*—L. S. M. and his great-great-great-grandson—are destined to death and the ensuing decay and rot that will happen (has happened) to their bodies. In both cases, all that will remain is the written words on the pages that they labored over during their lifetimes, and even these accomplishments will soon be nought but dust.

The only pair of actual blood-related brothers is, of course, Jean-Pierre and Jean-Marie, the regicide and the renegade, the revolutionary and the fugitive who abandoned the revolutionary cause:

> [...] like two incarnations of the same congenital spirit (or need) of rebellion, that is to say the younger [Jean-Marie] rebelling against this power, this authority which the elder one [Jean-Pierre] himself owed to an act of rebellion, both of them outlaws to a certain extent [...]. ([296], 437)

Jean-Marie is presented as Jean-Pierre's quasi twin, his double, and what is more, part of himself.[15] Jean-Pierre's crime consists not in his voting for the death of the king or even in helping pass the law against émigrés caught with arms in their possession, though the latter turns out to be tantamount to a death sentence imposed upon Jean-Marie. Rather Jean-Pierre's real crime is the murder of part of himself, "the other one who by the addition of a woman's name was in a way both male and female" ([293], 432). The last time the two brothers see each other alive, their quick, silent embrace, to which only Batti and the family dog are witness in the darkness of the fields near the family estate, is like an impossible situation in which a wild and a domestic animal meet for a brief instant near the fence that separates the farm from the forest. Interestingly, it is the androgynous Jean-Marie who is the wild one, the one who refuses to be shut in by the state-run bureaucracy of the military and political leaders of the

revolutionary government. Jean-Marie is compared to
the wild animal most feared and most hunted in eighteenth-century France, the wolf:

> [. . .] the wolf at bay, then, with the arrogance of the
> wild, untamed beast, his thin, nervous body, all sin-
> ewy under the ragged clothing, embodying at that
> instant [. . .] something more powerful than power:
> wild, haughty, with that look worse than hate or
> contempt: defiance, mockery, perhaps even pity for
> the other one, this double scarcely older than he
> [. . .]. ([293–94], 433)

This pair of brother enemies recalls Cain and Abel,
Romulus and Remus, or even Vergil and Simon, both
authors of their respective "Georgics." However, more
than any other couple in the novel, Jean-Marie and
Jean-Pierre symbolize the warring tension between
the female and male principles in Simon's fiction. One
recalls Simon's perennial *malaise* in dealing with female characters: the androcentrism of the point of view
and the sexism of the hero in *The Flanders Road,* as
well as the almost total inability of male characters to
communicate with women in *The Grass, Histoire, The
Battle of Pharsalus,* and *Conducting Bodies.*[16] In the
Simonian universe, men and women are like some ancestral enemies, never destined to understand or love
each other satisfactorily, as though they belonged to
different species. And whether the woman in question
is the figure of the mother or the beloved, she is fundamentally the inalterable Other who is as unattainable
as if she were always already in the grip of death. In
The Georgics, there are, to be sure, actual female characters: the matriarchal grandmother, the angelic

Marie-Anne, the poor widow Adélaïde, and the faithful but sterile Batti. But it is Jean-Marie who, like two earlier incarnations, Cécile in *The Wind* and Hélène in *Histoire,* embodies a kind of ideal, androgynous, even muscular femininity. Like many of Simon's other characters, Jean-Marie, the absent one, the fugitive running through the woods along with the other wild animals, is destined to be destroyed by a phallocratic society, that is, one ruled and dominated by the male principle and the concomitant values of order, hierarchy, and security.[17] In *The Georgics,* the lost paradise of sexual and psychological harmony between the sexes is evoked by a beautiful description of two butterflies mating, but it is also symbolized by the last nocturnal meeting of the very different L. S. M. brothers.

Couples are not limited, however, to actual or symbolic brothers in this novel, for the theme of brotherhood, of similarity and difference, of identity and contrast, is part of the larger phenomenon of textual analogy.[18] All of the many parallel structures which characterize this great novel could be legitimately considered as so many images of the archetypal Simonian couple as they are caught, reflected, and refracted from one end to the other across the length and breadth of this great *oeuvre,* as in some huge hall of mirrors.

NOTES

1. Cf. John Fletcher, "The General in *The Georgics,*" *The Review of Contemporary Fiction* 5.1 (1985): 100–03. A longer though still incomplete account of Lacombe-Saint-Michel's life is to be found in A.

Dry, *Soldats ambassadeurs sous le Directoire An IV-An VIII* (Paris: Plon, 1906), vol. 2, pp. 249–329.

2. Simon, "Essai de mise en ordre de notes prises au cours d'un voyage en Zeeland (1962) et complétées" (*Minuit* 3 [1973]: 1–18).

3. See Simon, *Discours de Stockholm,* pp. 12–15 and p. 23.

4. Intertextuality in *The Georgics* has been studied by numerous critics among whom the following should be cited: Alastair Duncan, "Claude Simon's *Les Géorgiques:* An Intertextual Adventure," *Romance Studies* 2 (1983): 90–107; Jean Duffy, "*Les Géorgiques* by Claude Simon: A Work of Synthesis and Renewal," *Australian Journal of French Studies* 21 (1984): 161–79; John Fletcher, "Intertextuality and Fictionality: *Les Géorgiques* and *Homage to Catalonia*" in *Claude Simon: New Directions,* ed. Duncan, pp. 100–12; Cora Reitsma-La Brujeere, "Récit et métarécit, texte et intertexte dans *Les Géorgiques* de Claude Simon," *French Forum* 9 (1984): 225–35. See also my forthcoming article, "Comment faire un cocktail simonien, ou *Les Géorgiques* relues et corrigées."

5. "Different climates, seasons, sounds, colors, darkness, light, the elements, food, noise, silence, movement, repose—all affect the bodily machine and consequently the mind" (Jean-Jacques Rousseau, *Confessions,* Book 9).

6. *The Georgics,* trans. Beryl and John Fletcher (London: Calder, 1989). *Les Géorgiques* (Paris: Minuit, 1981). Translations are my own. Page references to *The Georgics* appear in square brackets.

7. "The first pages of *The Georgics* show up the fictitiousness of the boundary that we sometimes like to imagine between fiction and its theory [. . .]" (Anthony Pugh, "From Drawing, to Painting, to Text: Claude Simon's Allegory of Representation and Reading in the Prologue to *The Georgics,*" *Review of Contemporary Fiction* 5.1 [1985]: 62).

8. Cf. Jean-Luc Seylaz, "Lecture du chapitre I des *Géorgiques,*" *L'Esprit créateur* 27.4 (1987): 80–88.

9. See Aline Baehler, "Aspects du personnage simonien: Corinne," *L'Esprit créateur* 27.4 (1987): 27–36.

10. *The World About Us,* p. 82; *Leçon de choses,* p. 123.

11. See Celia Britton, "Diversity of Discourse in Claude Simon's *Les Géorgiques,*" *French Studies* 38 (1984): 423–42.

12. Interestingly, L. S. M. met his future wife, Marie-Anne, at a

performance of the Gluck's opera and the Boy/Soldier hears Orpheus's lament, *"Dove andrò?"* from the same opera on the radio while at the front during World War II. As well, the sentence "And where will you go?" is to be found in a letter written by L. S. M. to a fellow officer. Furthermore, the story of Orpheus is related in Vergil's *Georgics*. Thus, it becomes clear that the Orpheus motif is a significant (inter)textual thread that holds Simon's novel together. See Michael Evans, "The Orpheus Myth in *Les Géorgiques*" in *Claude Simon: New Directions*, pp. 89–99.

13. Despite some similarities in their stories, L. S. M. is not to be confused with the first Reixach from *The Flanders Road*. Both were members of the Convention and were in Spain on military service. However, Reixach returned home and committed suicide, whereas Jean-Pierre L. S. M. spent a last peaceful year on his estate before dying of natural causes. In fact, an early reference to an L. S. M.-type character can be found in Simon's very first novel, *Le Tricheur* (Paris: Sagittaire, 1945), p. 68.

14. Cf. *The Georgics*, p. 20; *Les Géorgiques*, p. 28.

15. Cf. "And that brother! . . . That younger brother, the Chevalier, that ghost, nothing but a decaying carcass now, [. . .], that part of himself which for him [Jean-Pierre] had already begun to rot while still alive, from the moment when he had torn it out of himself, cut it off in an act of dreadful mutilation, like you tear out an eye, cut off a gangrenous limb, or in order to obey some biblical commandment, refusing not only to know him but excreting even his memory, never pronouncing, never writing *that name (Jean-Marie), which was in a sort of way the complement to his own (Jean-Pierre), only distinguished from it by the feminine ending, as though when they had been baptized someone had wanted to unite the two boys in one two-headed character,* [and] when speaking of him [. . .] designating him not by his Christian name, those syllables, *that group of familiar sounds which made him his own double,* but saying only 'my brother,' and that not only in his dealings with outsiders, not only in his own family [. . .] but even with Batti [. . .]." ([275], 404–05, my emphasis).

16. On the representation of female characters in Simon, see Britton, *Claude Simon: Writing the Visible,* pp. 167–68; Jean Duffy, "M(i)sreading Claude Simon: A Partial Analysis," *Forum for Mod-*

ern Languages 23.3 (1987): 228–40; and Winifred Woodhull, "Reading Claude Simon: Gender, Ideology, Representation," *L'Esprit créateur* 27.4 (1987): 5–16.

17. The secret police looking for O. when so-called enemies of the Spanish revolution are being rounded up and executed go by the name of "Security"!

18. See Michel Bertrand, *Langue romanesque et parole scripturale. Essai sur Claude Simon* (Paris: Presses Universitaires de France, 1987), pp. 154–56, 181–82; and Lucien Dällenbach, *"Les Géorgiques* ou la totalisation accomplie," *Critique* 414 (1981): 1226–42.

It is a difficult task to reach any definitive conclusions about a living author who continues to write. Despite his age Simon is still very much involved in his career as a writer. He appears to be in excellent health and is lively and alert with a mischievous sparkle in his bright blue eyes. As is often the case, the Nobel Prize slowed down his production; in fact he claims that the two most tiring episodes in his life were his World War II soldiering and the endless round of interviews and travel that followed the award of the famous prize. Nevertheless, Simon still finds time for his favorite activities: making collages, photography, and writing. Writing is hard work for Simon, and he has never sought to disguise the fact, an admission which some journalists have never seemed to understand. On the other hand, writing is Simon's life; it is his therapy, his play, his profession.

Although it is to be hoped that Simon will continue to produce, from the perspective of the late 1980s the general outline of his career is now clear to us. The quantity—twenty books written since World War II—is impressive in itself, but the radical changes that characterize the styles of Simon's writing over the years are even more striking. To be sure Simon does recycle material; no doubt the best example is Barcelona during the Spanish Civil War to which he has returned in five different books. But Simon never simply repeats himself; each of his novels, whatever the subject matter, has a unique configuration of thematic and narrative structure above and beyond the recurrence of familiar characters and obsessive leitmotifs.

The first four novels published from 1945 to 1957—*Le Tricheur, Gulliver, Le Sacre du printemps,* and *The Wind*—represent Simon's initial apprenticeship as a writer and as such they are somewhat derivative. At this stage in Simon's career he was still in the process of finding his own voice so that it is not surprising that these early works bear the mark of writers with whom the French novelist felt the greatest affinity, Dostoevsky and Faulkner.

Published during the late 1950s and 60s the five novels which make up the Reixach Cycle—*The Grass, The Flanders Road, The Palace, Histoire,* and *The Battle of Pharsalus*—correspond to the middle period of Simon's mature style. The ever-expanding fictive universe of these interlocking novels recalls Balzac's great novel cycle, *The Human Comedy,* whereas the care and skill with which Simon has crafted these verbally luxuriant texts recall Joyce. Despite the novels written since, it is still chiefly for these books that Simon is remembered. But Simon was not just some passing phenomenon of the 1960s French literary scene.

The 1970s saw the publication of three novels which proved that Simon was intent on breaking new fictional ground. However, these more impersonal narratives—*Conducting Bodies, Triptych,* and *The World About Us*—added to Simon's reputation of being a difficult writer more than any other of his books. In fact, these novels demonstrate an innovative and fresh approach to writing. The intricate verbal detail of these narratives can only enchance—not obscure—the fact

198

that they are grounded in the experiences, the sights, sounds, and smells of daily life.

Simon came back into critical favor with his longest and greatest novel, which combines techniques from both his second and third periods, *The Georgics.* Whether or not this novel initiated or constitutes in and of itself the fourth period in Simon's writing career is impossible to say at this point. What is certain is that *The Georgics,* along with *The Flanders Road* and *Histoire,* are some of the most important novels of modern French literature. They are all firmly anchored in the events of our century, while at the same time they manage to include the history of France and the West, not just as a backdrop to, but as an integral part of, the personal dramas of ordinary people. More than anything else, it is this process of textual weaving at both the individual and collective levels that makes these tales of modern Everymen so poignant.

What then is Simon's place in the literary hall of fame today? To be sure, his place *is* there, and it has been well earned even though some journalists have been loath to acknowledge the fact. Since 1972 some twenty-five books and collections of literary criticism have been published on Simon in French and English. Numerous articles and dissertations have been devoted to France's 1985 Nobel Laureate; one can hardly characterize Simon as an illustrious unknown any more. Plans are underway to make a movie based on *The Flanders Road,* and a German publisher recently brought out *Album d'un amateur,* a beautiful book of photographs with accompaning text, both by Simon. Major French publishing houses are scrambling to get books into print on a writer about whom little has been known in his own country. For it must be said that Simon's audience is worldwide, hardly limited to the literati of Paris. Simon himself claims that his greatest success has often been outside of France.

The trajectory of Simon's fame, or the lack of it, is not without irony. In the 1950s and 60s Alain Robbe-Grillet was the self-appointed leader and spokesperson of the French New Novel. In the 1970s Jean Ricardou took over this role and attempted to define who was in and who was out. Now it is he who is out of critical favor. During all this time Simon was content to work away patiently at his writing. Now in the 1980s one of the least aggressive members of the so-called New Novel school has won the Nobel, and another one, who was sometimes not even included in the list of approved writers, Marguerite Duras, has become an international best-selling author. But then such are the vagaries of the literary world.

Despite the 1985 Nobel, Simon has still not received the popular recognition his writing deserves either in France or America. Seven years after its original publication, *The Georgics* had still not yet appeared in English, and many of his books are not available in paperback or are simply not stocked by booksellers. Unfortunately the image of a difficult writer still persists, and given many readers' love of instant gratification and the easy-read, this all too often means that Simon is not known or read outside French departments. In fact, anyone who has read even one of Simon's novels knows that they are anything but dull. Of course they present a challenge, but then so does all art that has not been "assimilated," as Simon, after Proust, is fond of saying.

Simon undoubtedly deserves his place in the pantheon of French literature of the twentieth century along with Proust and Camus. In fact these writers' lives and careers intersect with Simon's in a special way. The first volume of Proust's *Remembrance of Things Past,* Simon's favorite novel, was published the very year that Simon and Camus were born, 1913. Both Camus and Simon wrote their first novels during World War II (Camus's *L'Etranger,* published in 1942; Simon's *Le Tricheur* in 1945). Of course, Camus's career peaked much earlier, for he won the Nobel Prize in 1957 just three years before his untimely death. Thus 1960 can seen as a watershed date marking the end of the existential novel, based on a socially and politically accepted message, which was so popular in the 1940s and 1950s. As well 1960 saw the publication of *The Flanders Road,* the first novel for which Simon won a literary prize and which really got his career as a novelist underway.

Unlike Camus, Simon's work does not seek to express a single message or even several. To be sure, his novels contain dominant themes (war, love, and death) but these are striking only for their very banality. Rather, meaning in Simon is indissociable from the structure of the writing itself, whether at the level of the phrase, the sentence, or the whole text. Like a magnificent collage or mosaic, Simon's *oeuvre* is there for all readers—not just literary critics—to appreciate and enjoy. The novels of Claude Simon are part and parcel of the modern tradition of our century with its penchant for fragmentation, self-reflexivity, quotation, and textual weaving. Indeed, seen from today's perspective, much more than the thematic concerns about time, memory, and consciousness which seemed crucial to critics in the 1960s, it is the all-important significance of language, of its infinite capacity for nuance and rhythm, for representation and wordplay, that unifies these works despite their individual differences. It is upon this, the wordsmith's craft of making beautiful things with words, that the reputation of Claude Simon the writer is justly based.

SELECTED BIBLIOGRAPHY

Works by Claude Simon

Fiction

Le Tricheur. Paris: Sagittaire [Minuit], 1945.

Gulliver. Paris: Calmann-Lévy, 1952.

Le Sacre du printemps. Paris: Calmann-Lévy, 1954.

Le Vent. Paris: Minuit, 1957. [*The Wind*. Trans. Richard Howard. New York: Braziller, 1959.]

L'Herbe. Paris: Minuit, 1958. [*The Grass*. Trans. Richard Howard. New York: Braziller, 1960.]

La Route des Flandres. Paris: Minuit, 1960. [*The Flanders Road,* Trans. Richard Howard. New York: Braziller, 1961.]

Le Palace. Paris: Minuit, 1962. [*The Palace*. Trans. Richard Howard. New York: Braziller, 1963.]

Femmes. On 23 paintings by Joan Miró. Paris: Editeur Maeght, 1966. Rpt. as *La Chevelure de Bérénice*. Paris: Minuit, 1983.

Histoire. Paris: Minuit, 1967. [*Histoire*. Trans. Richard Howard. New York: Braziller, 1968.]

La Bataille de Pharsale. Paris: Minuit, 1969. [*The Battle of Pharsalus*. Trans. Richard Howard. New York: Braziller, 1971.]

Orion aveugle. Geneva: Skira, 1970.

Les Corps conducteurs. Paris: Minuit, 1971. [*Conducting Bodies*. Trans. Helen R. Lane. New York: Viking, 1974.]

Triptyque. Paris: Minuit, 1973. [*Triptych*. Trans. Helen R. Lane. New York: Viking, 1976.]

Leçon de choses. Paris: Minuit, 1975. [*The World About Us*. Trans. Daniel Weissbort. Princeton, NJ: Ontario Review Press, 1983.]

Les Géorgiques. Paris: Minuit, 1981. [*The Georgics.* Trans. Beryl and John Fletcher. London: Calder, 1989.]

L'Invitation. Paris: Minuit, 1987.

L'Acacia. Paris: Minuit, 1989.

Selected Non-fiction

La Corde raide. Paris: Sagittaire [Minuit], 1947.

"Interview avec Claude Simon." Bettina L. Knapp. *Kentucky Romance Quarterly* 16.2 (1969): 179–90.

Introduction. *Orion aveugle.* By Simon. Geneva: Skira, 1970. [6–16].

"La Fiction mot à mot." *Nouveau roman: hier, aujourd'hui. 2. Pratiques.* Ed. Jean Ricardou and Françoise van Rossum-Guyon. Colloque au Centre culturel international de Cerisy-la-Salle du 20 au 30 juillet 1971. 2 vols. Paris: UGE, 1972. 2: 73–97. (Discussion 99–116.) ["Fiction Word by Word." Trans. Barbara Wright. *The Review of Contemporary Fiction* 5.1 (Spring 1985): 34–46.]

"Réponses de Claude Simon à quelques questions écrites de Ludovic Janvier." *Entretiens* 31 (1971): 15–29. ["Claude Simon's Answers to Some Questions Written by Ludovic Janvier." Trans. Barbara Wright. *Review of Contemporary Fiction* 5.1 (Spring 1985): 24–33.]

"Interview with Claude Simon." Claud DuVerlie, trans. J. Rogers and I. Rogers. *Sub-Stance* 8 (Winter 1974): 3–20.

"Claude Simon, à la question." Discussion with the participation of Claude Simon. Ricardou, *Claude Simon: analyse, théorie.* 403–31.

"Claude Simon: The Crossing of the Image." DuVerlie, trans. J. Rogers. *Diacritics* (Dec. 1977): 47–58.

"Simon on Simon: An Interview with the Artist." Randi Birn and Karen Gould, trans. Jane Carson. Birn and Gould, *Orion Blinded: Essays on Claude Simon.* 285–88.

"Roman, description et action." *Studi di letteratura francese* 8 (1982): 12-27.

"Interview with Claude Simon." Alastair B. Duncan. Duncan, *Claude Simon: New Directions*. 12–18.

"Interview with Claude Simon: Autobiography, the Novel, Politics." Anthony Cheal Pugh. *Review of Contemporary Fiction* 5.1 (Spring 1985): 4–13.

"Reflections on the Novel: Claude Simon's Address to the Colloquium on the New Novel, New York University, October 1982." Trans. Anthony Cheal Pugh. *Review of Contemporary Fiction* 5.1 (Spring 1985): 14–23. [Another translation of the same speech appears in *Three Decades of the French New Novel*. Ed. Lois Oppenheim. Urbana: U of Illinois P, 1986. 71–86.]

Discours de Stockholm. Paris: Minuit, 1986.

"The Novel as Textual Wandering: An Interview with Claude Simon." Claud DuVerlie. *Contemporary Literature* 28.1 (1987): 1–13.

Album d'un amateur. Remagen-Rolandseck: Rommerskirschen, 1988.

Critical Works

Bibliographies

Apeldoorn, Jo Van. "Bibliographie sélective." *Critique* 37.414 (nov. 1981): 1244–52.

"Bibliographie sélective." Établie par Gérard Roubichou et Alastair B. Duncan (1974) et mise à jour par Jan Baetens (1986). *Lire Claude Simon*. Ed. Jean Ricardou. Paris: Les Nouvelles Impressions, 1987. 432–62.

Dällenbach, Lucien. "Bibliographie critique." Dällenbach. *Claude Simon*. 213–17.

Duffy, Jean H. "Select Bibliography." Duncan, *Claude Simon, New Directions*. 156–64.

"Selected Bibliography." Birn and Gould. *Orion Blinded: Essays on Claude Simon*. 297–303.

Books

Bertrand, Michel. *Langue romanesque et parole scripturale: essai sur Claude Simon*. Paris: PUF, 1987. Uses the terminology of French theorist Jean Ricardou to study *La Bataille de Pharsale, Les Corps conducteurs, Triptyque,* and *Les Géorgiques* as examples of textual writing.

Britton, Celia. *Claude Simon: Writing the Visible*. Cambridge Studies in French. Cambridge: Cambridge UP, 1987. Seeks to correct "a certain misrecognition of the presence of the visible" in Simon's writing. Makes use of the ideas of French psychoanalyst Jacques Lacan to study the tension between representational and antirepresentational elements in Simon's novels from 1958 to 1981 (quotations in French and English).

Carroll, David. *The Subject in Question: The Language of Theory and the Strategies of Fiction*. Chicago: U of Chicago P, 1982. Using Simon's novels from 1954 to 1973 as case-studies, the author examines the "confrontation" between literary texts and various modern theories (structuralism, linguistics, Marxism, historiography, formalism).

Dällenbach, Lucien. *Claude Simon*. Les Contemporains 1. Paris: Seuil, 1988. The best introduction in French, written from a post-structuralist perspective; a veritable mine of resource materials, including photographs and an unpublished interview.

Evans, Michael. *Claude Simon and the Transgressions of Modern Art*. London: Macmillan, 1988. Very detailed analysis of questions of intertextuality, textual framing, and self-reflexivity in novels published between 1960 and 1981 (quotations in French and English.)

Fletcher, John. *Claude Simon and Fiction Now*. London: Calder, 1975. Adopts a comparative approach to Simon's novels from 1958 to 1969 and novels by four other modern writers.

Gould, Karen. *Claude Simon's Mythic Muse.* Columbia, SC: French Literature Publications, 1979. Describes mythological images and themes in *The Flanders Road, Histoire,* and *The Battle of Pharsalus.*

Jiménez-Fajardo, Salvador. *Claude Simon.* Boston: Twayne, 1975. A detailed introduction to each of Simon's novels from *The Wind* to *Triptych,* with emphasis on plot and theme.

Kadish, Doris Y. *Practices of the New Novel in Claude Simon's "L'Herbe" and "La Route des Flandres."* Fredericton, New Brunswick: York, 1979. A detailed study of two novels, with emphasis on plot, character, description, and point of view.

Loubère, J. A. E. *The Novels of Claude Simon.* Ithaca: Cornell UP, 1975. A general but thorough study of Simon's fiction, from *The Wind* to *Triptych.*

Neumann, Guy A. *Echos et correspondances dans "Triptyque" et "Leçon de choses" de Claude Simon.* Lausanne: L'Age d'Homme, 1983. A minutious study of two of Simon's later works.

Pugh, Anthony Cheal. *Simon: "Histoire".* London: Grant, 1982. An excellent monograph on one of Simon's most complex novels (quotations in French).

Roubichou, Gérard. *Lecture de "L'Herbe" de Claude Simon.* Lausanne: L'Age d'Homme, 1976. A 300-page study of Simon's 1958 novel. Excellent analysis of point of view, as well as of stylistic and narrative structures.

Sarkonak, Ralph. *Claude Simon: les carrefours du texte.* Toronto: Paratexte, 1986. A study of Simon's fiction, principally *Histoire* and *La Bataille de Pharsale;* adopts a semiotic approach.

Storrs, Neal. *Liquid: A Source of Meaning and Structure in Claude Simon's "La Bataille de Pharsale".* New York: Lang, 1983. Studies the unifying function of liquid at thematic, stylistic and narrative levels of Simon's 1969 novel (quotations in French).

207

Sykes, Stuart. *Les romans de Claude Simon*. Paris: Minuit, 1979. A general study of Simon's fiction from *Le Vent* to *Leçon de choses*. Includes diagrams to illustrate narrative structures.

Collectives

Birn, Randi and Karen Gould, eds. *Orion Blinded: Essays on Claude Simon*. Lewisburg: Bucknell UP, 1981.

Brewer, Mária Minich, ed. *Claude Simon*. Special issue of *L'Esprit créateur* 27.4 (Winter 1987).

Duncan, Alastair B., ed. *Claude Simon, New Directions: Collected Papers*. Edinburgh: Scottish Academic Press, 1985.

DuVerlie, Claud and Christiane P. Makward, eds. Special issue of *Sub-Stance* 8 (Winter 1974).

MLN (Claude Simon Colloquium) 103.4 (1988): 711–81.

Review of Contemporary Fiction 5.1 (Spring 1985).

Ricardou, Jean, ed. *Claude Simon: analyse, théorie*. Actes du colloque qui s'est tenu à Cerisy-la-Salle du 1er au 8 juillet 1974. Paris: UGE, 1975. Rpt. as *Lire Claude Simon*. Paris: Les Nouvelles Impressions, 1987.

Roelens, Maurice. *Claude Simon*. Special issue of *Cahiers de l'Université de Perpignan* 1 (Fall 1986).

Séguier, Marcel, ed. *Claude Simon*. Special issue of *Entretiens* 31 (1972).

Sur Claude Simon. Paris: Minuit, 1987.

La Terre et la guerre dans l'oeuvre de Claude Simon. Special issue of *Critique* 37.414 (nov. 1981): 1147–1252.

Vidal, Jean-Pierre, ed. *Claude Simon*. Special issue of *Etudes littéraires* 9.1 (avril 1976): 5–221.

General and Comparative Articles

Brewer, Mária Minich. "An Energetics of Reading: Intertextual in Claude Simon." *Romanic Review* 73.4 (Nov. 1982): 489–504.

————. "Claude Simon: The Critical Properties of Painting." *Review of Contemporary Fiction* 5.1 (Spring 1985): 104–09.

Britton, Celia. "Claude Simon's Generation Game: The Family and the Text." Duncan, *Claude Simon, New Directions*. 19–29.

————. "Visual Effects by Claude Simon." *Paragraph* 10 (1987): 45–64.

Carroll, David. "Narrative Poetics and the Crisis in Culture: Claude Simon's Return to 'History'." *L'Esprit créateur* 27.4 (Winter 1987): 48-60.

Dällenbach, Lucien. "Mise en abyme et redoublement spéculaire chez Claude Simon." Ricardou, *Claude Simon: analyse, théorie*. 151–71 (discussion 172–90).

————. "La Question primordiale." *Sur Claude Simon*. Paris: Minuit, 1987. 63–93.

————. "L'Archive simonienne." *MLN* 103.4 (1988): 736–50.

Doubrovsky, Serge. "Notes sur la genèse d'une écriture." *Entretiens* 31 (1972): 51–64.

Duffy, Jean H. "Art as Defamiliarisation in the Theory and Practice of Claude Simon." *Romance Studies* 2 (Summer 1983): 108–23.

————. "M(i)sreading Claude Simon: A Partial Analysis." *Forum for Modern Language Studies* 23.3 (1987): 228–40.

Duncan, Alastair B. "Claude Simon and William Faulkner." *Forum for Modern Language Studies* [St. Andrews, Scotland] 9.3 (July 1973): 235–52.

————. "Claude Simon: la crise de la représentation." *Critique* 37.414 (nov. 1981): 1181–1200.

DuVerlie, Claud. *"Amor interruptus:* The Question of Eroticism or, Eroticism in Question in the Works of Claude Simon." Trans. J. Dickson. *Sub-Stance* 8 (Winter 1974): 21–33.

Jiménez-Fajardo, Salvador. "Claude Simon and Latin American Fiction: Some Common Grounds." Birn and Gould, *Orion Blinded: Essays on Claude Simon*. 248–59.

Makward, Christiane P. "Claude Simon: Earth, Death and

Eros." *Sub-Stance* 8 (Winter 1974): 35–43.

———. "Aspects of Bisexuality in Claude Simon's Works." Birn and Gould, *Orion Blinded: Essays on Claude Simon.* 219–35.

Pugh, Anthony Cheal. "Claude Simon: The Narrator and his Double." *Twentieth Century Studies* 6 (Dec. 1971): 30–40.

Riffaterre, Michael. "Orion voyeur: L'Écriture intertextuelle de Claude Simon." *MLN* 103.4 (1988): 711–35.

Sykes, Stuart W. "'Mise en abyme' in the Novels of Claude Simon." *Forum for Modern Language Studies* [St. Andrews, Scotland] 9.4 (Oct. 1973): 333–45.

———. "Ternary Form in Three Novels by Claude Simon." *Symposium* 32 (Spring 1978): 25–40.

———. "Parmi les aveugles le borgne est roi: A Personal Survey of Simon Criticism." Duncan, *Claude Simon: New Directions.* 140–55.

Woodhull, Winifred. "Reading Claude Simon: Gender, Ideology, Representation." *L'Esprit créateur* 27.4 (Winter 1987): 5–16.

Articles on Specific Novels by Claude Simon

The Wind

Bjurström, Carl Gustaf. "Lecture de Claude Simon: *Le Vent.*" *Critique* 37.414 (nov. 1981): 1151–66.

Duffy, Jean H. "Meaning and Subversion in Simon's *Le Vent:* Some Structural Considerations." *French Studies Bulletin* 15 (Summer 1985): 8–10.

The Grass

Dällenbach, Lucien. "L'Abyssal et le circulaire (*L'Herbe*)." *Le Récit spéculaire: Essai sur la mise en abyme.* Paris: Seuil, 1977. 171–73.

Holter, Karin. "La constance difficile." Ricardou, *Claude Simon: analyse, théorie.* 368–75.

Van Buuren, Maarten. "L'Essence des choses: étude de la description dans l'œuvre de Claude Simon." *Poétique* 43 (sept. 1980): 324–33.

The Flanders Road

Dällenbach, Lucien. "Le Tissu de mémoire." *La Route des Flandres.* Collection "Double." Paris: Minuit, 1982. 297–316.

Higgins, Lynn A. "Gender and War Narrative in *La Route des Flandres.*" *L'Esprit créateur* 27.4 (Winter 1987): 17–26.

Lanceraux, Dominique. "Modalités de la narration dans *La Route des Flandres.*" *Poétique* 4.14 (1973): 235–49.

Prince, Gerald. "How to Redo Things With Words: *La Route des Flandres.*" *MLN* 103.4 (1988): 769–81.

Ricardou, Jean. "Un Ordre dans la débacle." *Problèmes du nouveau roman.* Paris: Seuil, 1967. 44–55. [Originally published in *Critique* 16 (déc. 1960): 1011-24.]

Le Palace

Kadish, Doris Y. "From the Narration of Crime to the Crime of Narration: Claude Simon's *Le Palace.*" *International Fiction Review* 4 (1977): 128-36.

Solomon, Philip H. "Flights of Time Lost: Bird Imagery in Claude Simon's *Le Palace.*" *Twentieth Century French Fiction: Essays for Germaine Brée.* Ed. George Stambolian. New Brunswick, NJ: Rutgers UP, 1975. 166–83.

Sykes, Stuart. "Tintin faisant la révolution? Novel Attitudes to the Spanish Civil War." *Romance Studies* 3 (1983): 122–35.

Vidal, Jean-Pierre. *"Le Palace,* palais des mirages intestins ou, L'Auberge espagnole." *Etudes Littéraires* 9.1 (avril 1976): 189–214.

Histoire

Kelly, Lynda Harper. "Spatial Composition and Formal Harmonies in Claude Simon's *Histoire*." *Modern Language Studies* 9.1 (Winter 1978–1979): 73-83.

Pugh, Anthony Cheal. "Invitation à une lecture polyvalente." Ricardou, *Claude Simon: analyse, théorie.* 387–94.

Roubichou, Gérard. *"Histoire* or The Serial Novel." Trans. Jane Carson. Birn and Gould, *Orion Blinded: Essays on Claude Simon.* 173–83.

Rousset, Jean. *"Histoire* de Claude Simon: le jeu des cartes postales." *Versants. Revue suisse des littératures romanes* 1 (nov. 1981): 121–33. [Also published in *Studi di letteratura francese* 8 (1982): 28–33.]

Starobinski, Jean. "La journée dans *Histoire.*" *Sur Claude Simon.* Colloque. Paris: Minuit, 1987. 7–32.

The Battle of Pharsalus

Birn, Randi. "Proust, Claude Simon and the Art of the Novel." *Papers on Language and Literature* 13.2 (1977): 168–86.

Gosselin, Claudia Hoffer. "Voices of the Past in Claude Simon's *La Bataille de Pharsale.*" *Intertextuality, New Perspectives in Criticism.* Ed. Jeanine Parisier Plottel and Hanna Charney. New York: New York Literary Forum, 1978. 23–33.

Ricardou, Jean. "La Bataille de la phrase." *Pour une théorie du nouveau roman.* Paris: Seuil, 1971. 118–58. [Originally published in *Critique* 26 (mars 1970): 226–56.]

Rossum-Guyon, Françoise van. "De Claude Simon à Proust: un exemple d'intertextualité." *Lettres Nouvelles* 4 (sept.-oct. 1972): 107–37. [Originally published in "Un Nouveau

nouveau roman?" Special issue of *Marche romane* 21.1–2 (1971): 71–92.]

Rousset, Jean. "La Guerre en peinture." *Critique* 37.414 (nov. 1981): 1201-10.

Conducting Bodies

Duffy, Jean H. "The Textualization of Time in *Conducting Bodies, Triptych* and *The World About Us*." *Review of Contemporary Fiction* 5.1 (Spring 1985): 71–76.

DuVerlie, Claud. "Pictures for Writing: Premises for a Graphopictology." Birn and Gould, *Orion Blinded: Essays on Claude Simon*. 200–18.

Janvier, Ludovic. "On Body-Circuits." Trans. Robin Knee and Mary E. Wolf. *Review of Contemporary Fiction* 5.1 (Spring 1985): 77–84.

Raillon, Jean-Claude. "Eléments d'une physique littérale." *Degrés* 1.4 (oct. 1973): g1-g29.

Triptych

Andrews, Mark. "Formalist Dogmatism, Derridean Questioning, and the Return of Affect: Towards a Distributed Reading of *Triptyque*." *L'Esprit créateur* 27.4 (Winter 1987): 37–47.

Dällenbach, Lucien. "La Fin des illusions totalisantes (*Triptyque*)." *Le Récit spéculaire: Essai sur la mise en abyme*. Paris: Seuil, 1977. 193–200.

Jost, François. "Claude Simon: topographies de la description et du texte." *Critique* 30.330 (nov. 1974): 1031–40.

Lotringer, Sylvère. "Cryptique." Ricardou, *Claude Simon: analyse, théorie*. 313–33 (discussion 334–47).

Pugh, Anthony Cheal. "Du *Tricheur* à *Triptyque*, et inversement." *Etudes littéraires* 9.1 (avril 1976): 137–60.

The World About Us

Dragonetti, Roger. "Leçon de choses et Le son de choses." *MLN* 103.4 (1988): 751–68.

Evans, Michael. "Two Uses of Intertextuality: References to Impressionist Painting and *Madame Bovary* in Claude Simon's *Leçon de choses*." *Nottingham French Studies* 19.1 (May 1980): 33–45.

Gaudin, Colette. "Niveaux de lisibilité dans *Leçon de choses* de Claude Simon." *Romanic Review* 68.3 (May 1977): 175–96.

Raillard, Georges. "Le rythme des choses." *Critique* 37.414 (nov. 1981): 1167–80.

The Georgics

Britton, Celia. "Diversity of Discourse in Simon's *Les Géorgiques*." *French Studies* [Oxford] 38.4 (1984): 423–42.

Dällenbach, Lucien. *"Les Géorgiques* ou, La Totalisation accomplie." *Critique* 37.414 (nov. 1981): 1226–42.

Duffy, Jean H. *"Les Géorgiques* by Claude Simon: A Work of Synthesis and Renewal." *Australian Journal of French Studies* 21 (1984): 161–79.

Duncan, Alastair B. "Claude Simon's *Les Géorgiques:* An Intertextual Adventure." *Romance Studies* 2 (Summer 1983): 90–107.

Fletcher, John. "Intertextuality and Fictionality: *Les Géorgiques* and *Homage to Catalonia*." Duncan, *Claude Simon: New Directions*. 100–12.

Pugh, Anthony Cheal. "Facing the Matter of History: *Les Géorgiques*." Duncan, *Claude Simon: New Directions*. 113–30.